THE GREAT COSMIC LESSON PLAN

*Healing through spirituality,
humor and music*

By Sam Menahem, Ph.D.

BALBOA.
PRESS

A DIVISION OF HAY HOUSE

Balboa Press books may be ordered through booksellers or by contacting:

Balboa Press
A Division of Hay House
1663 Liberty Drive
Bloomington, IN 47403
www.balboapress.com
1 (877) 407-4847

Because of the dynamic nature of the Internet, any web addresses or links contained in this book may have changed since publication and may no longer be valid. The views expressed in this work are solely those of the author and do not necessarily reflect the views of the publisher, and the publisher hereby disclaims any responsibility for them.

The author of this book does not dispense medical advice or prescribe the use of any technique as a form of treatment for physical, emotional, or medical problems without the advice of a physician, either directly or indirectly. The intent of the author is only to offer information of a general nature to help you in your quest for emotional and spiritual well-being. In the event you use any of the information in this book for yourself, which is your constitutional right, the author and the publisher assume no responsibility for your actions.

Any people depicted in stock imagery provided by Thinkstock are models, and such images are being used for illustrative purposes only.
Certain stock imagery © Thinkstock.

Print information available on the last page.

ISBN: 978-1-5043-2891-3 (sc)
ISBN: 978-1-5043-2892-0 (hc)
ISBN: 978-1-5043-2890-6 (e)

Library of Congress Control Number: 2015935027

Balboa Press rev. date: 3/18/2015

CONTENTS

PART TWO
HANS OFF: THE PSYCHOLOGIST

INTRODUCTION

As a psychologist with forty years of experience, I have spent a great deal of time helping patients delve into some very basic existential questions:

Is life just a random series of events, and when you die you cease to exist? Or is life some sort of well-orchestrated, meaningful lesson, designed for each person's learning and edification? If the latter is true, what are we supposed to be learning? Is it a test? Is there some sort of omnipotent God administering this test? Is God some sort of proctor, timing us, waiting to see if we get the right answer? If so, what is the right answer? What is the meaning of life? What happens when you die? Is there anything "after" our mortal existence? Is there some sort of reward for getting the right answer? Do we go to some kind of heaven if we get it right? Do we go to purgatory or hell if we get it wrong?

I have long been asking myself the same questions.

My life has been a constant search for meaning and answers. Helping others grapple with the answers has helped me, too. The title of this book and first chapter, "The Great Cosmic Lesson Plan" is based on a piece I wrote for a journal called, "Pure Inspiration" several decades ago. It was inspired by a question asked by my nine-year-old daughter, twenty-two years ago. The various ensuing chapters reflect my answers to basic spiritual and existential questions.

I have found my answers through living, helping others and learning from great teachers. As you will see in the pages ahead, I have learned from so many sources, including the great religions of Judaism, Christianity, Buddhism, Taoism and Hinduism. All religions try to grapple with existential issues: meaning, death, responsibility, and isolation. There is no doubt that religion has been helpful to me, but I needed more. I have long loved psychology and philosophy, and have also learned a lot from great philosophers and psychologists like Drs. Victor Frankl (my professor in graduate school), Sigmund Feud, Carl Jung, Karen Horney and Thomas Hora. My favorite philosophers include Plato, Emerson and Kierkegaard. I have also learned a lot from modern psycho-spiritual philosophies including *The Seth Material* by Jane Roberts and *A Course in Miracles*. Most importantly, I have learned from the events of my life.

Part one includes essays I've written for other publications, and my own personal stories. I also share how illness helped me grow, including; rheumatic fever at age nine and a nearly fatal heart attack at fifty-five. All of the most painful events of my life have taught me a lot about life. Life is supposed to be fun, but not all fun. We are supposed to have some pain, just enough to prod us into becoming the best possible human being we can be. We are supposed to become as loving, forgiving, kind, generous and helpful as possible. We are supposed to place God, and the goodness of God above all else. In times of trouble, we are supposed to turn to a transcendent God for strength and guidance. All religions, including Judaism, Christianity, Buddhism, Hinduism, and Taoism all assert that we should center our lives in spirituality. Why do we become so embroiled in everyday existence that we forget about God and spiritual values? Perhaps it is this very absorption in material living that impedes up from living primarily for spiritual reasons. Each chapter has been designed to wake up a different portion of our basic humanness and spirituality. I have concluded that we are embarked on a great cosmic lesson plan. Or is it a great *"comic"* lesson plan?

Humor is very important to our coping with everyday physical reality and eventually transcending it. This is why Part Two is a novelette, a comic exploration of life through the eyes of a fictional character, Dr. Hans Off, a chiropractor who has to give up his profession after being bitten on the hand by an aardvark. Since his hand is paralyzed, he can no longer practice chiropractic. So he starts a new career as a psychoanalyst. Strangely, he notices that all of his patients are very unusual, almost like fictional characters from TV. On top of that, he starts hearing voices, claiming to be historical figures. So he goes to an analyst, Dr. Otto B. Anal. Dr. Off's experiences with three different therapists are humorous but also meaningful. He takes us on a trip through the history and systems of psychology. He starts with a psychoanalyst, then goes to an existentialist and finally finds his answers by developing his spirituality. Let us begin the journey toward healing and wholeness.

PART ONE

CHAPTER 1

The Great Cosmic Lesson Plan

"Hey dad, what is life for anyway? It's not that much fun." This question was posed by my nine-year old daughter Lauren. We were riding in the car, on the way to a "biddy basketball" game (a children's league). I guess she wasn't enjoying the games too much. But I didn't know the exact reason for her question. Somehow, at that moment, she was wondering what life is all about and I had to respond. I replied with the first answer that popped into my head, "Life is about loving, as many people as you can…as often as you can."

The second part of her statement about fun gave me a clue about how to continue. "You are right: nobody has fun all the time," I told her. "You do have fun sometimes don't you?" She admitted that was true. I continued. "But if you love people as much as you can, you will be happy. That is the most important thing in life, love people and you will be happy." We then went on to the game and the question was dropped. My daughter has grown up into a happy young woman, who has her share of fun, with occasional doses of negative events and issues. No more than anyone else, less than others. I sometimes wonder if she even remembers that conversation. My guess is no. But from my observations, she is a very loving person, so she followed my advice. She is learning her life lessons in her own way.

Still, is that enough of an answer to a question that has perplexed human beings since time immemorial? Maybe it sounds too trite or pat to an adult who is battling serious illness, financial ruin or a puzzling series of failures. Just love everyone. Some might be thinking: "Yeah right, I'm going to love my husband who just cheated on me and left me." Or, "Sure, I'll just love everyone while I die of cancer or heart disease." "Well, my house just floated away in a hurricane, but I'll just love everyone and it will be all right." In short, there is a lot of resistance to accepting a life that is full of problems, issues and seemingly negative events. People often get discouraged, depressed, and filled with self-pity and anger when things don't go their way. What is there to say without being banal or trite?

Bad Things, Good People

I give many speeches. During these talks, I often ask the audience two questions. First, "How many people here think they are a good person?" Everyone, of course, raises their hand. Then I ask, "How many people here have had at least one bad thing happen to them?" After a few snickers, of course, everyone raises their hand again. I then pronounce, "Now you know why Rabbi (Harold) Kushner sold so many copies of his book, *When Bad Things Happen to Good People.*" Bad things happen to all people." The question we ask ourselves in times of distress shouldn't be, "Why me?" It should be:

"Why not me?"

Rabbi Kushner might even agree with that statement. However, we seem to have different concepts of God. He portrays God as a wonderful, but overworked parent, with many children, running around, putting out fires. God is very busy, says Rabbi Kushner, sometimes he slips up, and bad things happen. This is how the Rabbi counters the erroneous concept that bad things happen as a punishment for being bad. Indeed, bad things also happen to good, righteous people. However, I think he misses the mark with the overworked parent metaphor. There must be some other reason so many "bad" things happen to all people. Of course, people are not all bad or all good. Most of us try our best to live a good and righteous life. All of us, however, have the potential to do some hurtful things. Psychologically, this is called our "shadow." So are the bad events of our life the result of unknown bad deeds? Or repressed shadow emotions? Are we being punished for real or imagined thoughts and actions? I think not. The punishment metaphor just does not hold up for me. I just do not see God as a vengeful judge or a beleaguered parent. I will explore in more depth the differences between Rabbi Kushner's philosophy and mine in a later chapter.

Atheists have a different view of why things happen the way they do, randomness. My scientific, materialist friends might jump in and say, "Why are you trying to make sense out of meaningless events? Stuff just happens. Why not just accept your life and do the best you can? Why do you have to make up a supernatural God that punishes or saves? Just suck it up and make the best of your life before you die and are obliterated." Whew! To me, that is a very depressing pathway. In order to go down that path, you have to be very cynical. You have to ignore the many wonderful qualities of all being. You have to ignore all selfless acts of love, all beauty, chocolate, ice cream, wisdom, and baseball, the very essence of how life may have started in the first place. Was life started by a random big bang, followed by chaos? I don't think so.

I remember Dr. Victor Frankl (a holocaust survivor and psychiatrist) once said, vociferously, in our class, "Life must have some meaning." What could be the meaning of all the suffering we go through on Earth? Randomness obviates meaning. Thus, I long ago rejected the purely scientific, materialist, random, no God theory. But my search for meaning continued by studying philosophy. Was there anywhere else to look for meaning in the history of philosophy? That's when I discovered the doctrine of existentialism.

The Question of Why

Existentialist philosophers, such as John Paul Sartre and Soren Kierkegaard, try to determine why things happen as they do. Sartre, an atheist and communist, felt there was no God but there was meaning.

He argued that man [humans?] must create his own meaning by taking responsibility for his own thoughts, feelings and behavior. This is an interesting amalgam of atheism and New Age thinking. I like the part about taking responsibility and creating your own reality. However, the atheist part denies any context for this meaning. He seems to be saying you just live, making the best of any bad things that happen to you. Then, you die and are obliterated. He recommends being courageous, responsible, and reasonable- all good ideas, then… you die. When you are dead, you are completely gone — that is it.

Kierkegaard put existentialism in a religious (Christian) context. He felt that human beings go through three stages: pleasure seeking, ethical/moral standards and religious belief. In the first stage, we are purely pleasure seekers, narcissists (are you listening Freud?). Eventually, we realize that there is more to life than pursuing pleasure and avoiding pain. There is an ethical- moral dimension to life. We try to do the right thing, just because it is right. There is no supernatural reason for doing so. We just do it. Finally, there is the opening up of a religious dimension. Western religions assert that there is a God and we do the right things to please him. Also we fear his wrath if we are bad. That, of course, takes us back to the original problem with a monotheistic model of God, already discussed with Rabbi Kushner's philosophy. Thus, both atheistic and religious forms of existentialism still leave us floundering.

Personally, I was still looking for meaning at the time my daughter asked me that big question. My daughter's question was still not completely answered by existential thought. In the narcissistic stage of pure pleasure seeking (childhood-where most of our modern culture is), we develop self-pity when bad things happen. We see no meaning in ill fortune. Even in a monotheistic belief system we find only the idea that we are being punished or are not important enough for God to help us. There must be a better way of looking at life. I still had questions:

> Could God be something other than a Santa Claus figure, punishing bad deeds and rewarding good deeds?

Could it be that the real God is not a comic book superhero supposed to rescue us, like Superman rescues Lois Lane?

Could the narcissistic idea that nothing bad should ever happen to us on Earth be mistaken?

Could it be that we have to learn something from our sufferings on the planet Earth?

Could it be that the real God is trying to teach us something that we can only learn by learning how to cope better with the difficulties of an Earthly life?

Yes, of course, to all of these questions. In fact, from these questions I had formulated an answer:

Life on Earth is a gigantic lesson plan from God! This is the great cosmic lesson plan.

Any teacher knows that each lesson must be taught through a lesson plan. This plan must have an aim and a method.

The aim of the great cosmic lesson plan is, (drum roll please)...

To discover the true nature of Oneness with God, to become fully aware and experience the Oneness, preferably, while still ensconced in a human, physical body.

How will we know if we have succeeded? That is easy. Enlightened beings are kind, loving, forgiving, non-judgmental, happy, peaceful and humble. All they want to do while still in a body is to help others gain the same level of enlightenment. Think of the Dalai Lama, Mother Teresa and Mahatma Ghandi.

Methodology of the Lesson Plan

I have concluded that life is set up so that human ego consciousness will *appear to be* separate from God. Each individual will totally identify with the body and separate ego. Due to this universal error, God will be viewed as either a savior, enemy, dysfunctional parent or completely non-existent. Death will be both feared and desired as a way out of suffering. The unconscious desire to die as an "escape hatch" will be repressed and denied by most people. Thus, most people will fear death except those few who are aware of desiring it as an escape from suffering.

This hellish period will continue until we realize that we need to *experience God the way God really is*. God is not a comic book superhero. God is not judging us. God does not get angry. **God is a Spiritual Oneness characterized by love, peace, power and intelligence.** God is just waiting for the "teachable moment" for each fragment of himself (humans) who have gotten lost in materialism, to realize and experience the Oneness that is all there is!

This "aha" experience may be accomplished by prayer, meditation or a simple "awakening" to the philosophy of Monism, aka the "Spirituality of Oneness." It is the answer to the question, "what is the meaning of life?" All events, especially the seemingly bad ones, are opportunities to turn to our real self or inner teacher and ask, "What is going on here? What do I have to learn from this so that I may become more peaceful, kind, loving and accepting, ultimately becoming a spiritual being?"

Chuck's Story

Chuck came into psychotherapy complaining of depression, inertia and marital dysfunction. His wife, a very successful sales person, continually complained about his passivity, low energy and refusal to do simple things like open the mail or take care of his body. He told me that he has a severe case of diabetes and needs insulin, as well as careful control of his diet. He was very lackadaisical about his need to manage his blood sugar. His wife got enraged over this. He just shrugged and became more withdrawn and depressed. I explained to Chuck that his passive-aggressive, resistant behavior served many functions for him. First, it enabled him to get his wife angry. Then she punished him by yelling at him. Thus, he had a guilty, victim, self-concept, which **required** punishment. This negative self-concept would be strengthened. He saw himself as a victim of everything from his disease to his wife's anger. He was suffering from victim thinking and unworthiness. His primary way of dealing with life was by being passive-aggressive. Passive- aggressive behavior is completely unconscious. Thus, the motto of the passive-aggressive person is, *"what did I do* to deserve this? (why should I be criticized and yelled at)."The unconscious passivity is designed to annoy the other person.

Chuck needed a context to understand what he was doing to bring on and exacerbate his suffering. I pointed out to him that diabetes is sometimes called "accelerated aging" by the medical community. Physically, the pancreas shuts down, there is no insulin, and cells age and die rapidly. Was he unconsciously hastening his own death? He admitted that he believed that when we die, there is nothing. Thus, to him, death was an "escape hatch" from the endless suffering caused by his physical condition and his unconscious, angry refusal to take responsibility for his life. Some people might say I am blaming the victim here. I think not. Even though he did not consciously order diabetes, he was conscious of welcoming death whenever it came. He was also aware that he did not manage his diabetes well, thus hastening the process of death, which would free him from having to face his responsibilities. If he decided to take responsibility for his life, manage his illness, open the mail, and make choices for happier thoughts, feelings and behaviors, he could live, longer, happier and better.

He was quite distressed at first, when I suggested that death might not be the end of everything. I told him I believed that life continues after physical death. If he died in a depressed state of mind, he might have to go through more suffering (the "life review" in which you feel all your feelings and those you induced in others) until he saw the light. Then he might have to reincarnate and try again to get the most from his new lesson plan. But, I stated enthusiastically, there is good news: If he took responsibility and became happier, he could be released from suffering now! Then, at physical death, he might see the light right away and become one with the higher power we call God. It is not physical death that brings us enlightenment. It is getting the point of the great cosmic lesson plan. *Take responsibility for your life now. Be here now! Be loving now! Only love is real!* (I hear Carol King singing in the background)

At first, he was angry at me for taking away his "escape hatch" of suicide if life was too difficult. But he is now taking steps toward fulfilling his lesson plan in his own way. He needs to express love for himself now. He is managing his illness better by exercising, opening his mail, making plans, traveling and doing interesting things. He is getting along better with his wife. He is looking at his life more humorously. He is no longer depressed or suicidal. He is cooperating with his version of the great cosmic lesson plan. Understanding and accepting Oneness with divinity is a big step for him to take. He is getting it, slowly. Death is not the answer. Love, humor and connecting with others and universal Oneness is the answer.

Chuck's life is clearly improving as he follows the lesson plan of his life. We all need to let go of fear, anger and guilt that come from accepting our separated (from divinity) material life as all there is. As we gradually let go of the painful emotions of fear, anger and guilt our life improves. That does not mean that we just sail smoothly through the rest of our life, it just means that we perceive things differently. We accept the good and bad events of our life as part of our unique lesson plan, leading us to self and God realization.

Hannah's Story

A colleague in my office referred Hannah to me. He felt she needed a sympathetic ear, and that we would be a good match, since she was a religious Jew and I am also Jewish. Since she was over 90, he was not expecting great changes. At first, it seemed that pure empathy was the only recourse. Week after week, her anxiety went out of control over small things. I would calm her down and she would leave feeling better, temporarily. She frequently reported that inevitably, on Thursday night, after we had our weekly session, something very weird would happen, something upsetting to her. Most people would call these events small things. For example, she would get a letter telling her she had won a lot of money. Though I would repeatedly tell her that these were scams, she would insist on calling the scammers back and getting upset when they wanted her to send money to them first. "Just ignore these scams," I urged her. But no, she had to inquire and get upset. She was plagued by anxiety and worry about the future.

One week, she came in upset because a medical claim for her eye doctor was rejected. "What if I have to pay it?" she said. I asked to see the letter. "It seems that the claim was rejected because you are dead," I replied. I used a line straight from Mark Twain: "Just call them and tell them the reports of your death were greatly exaggerated." "But doctor," she replied, "What if they don't listen? Why do these things keep happening to me?" I paused and mentioned the title of this book. Then I asked her: "What if all these things happen because life is a great lesson plan? You have to learn to control your anxiety, focus on God, ask for the strength and calmness to take care of these small things in a matter of fact way, let go and move on." This calmed her momentarily as the session ended.

The next week, she appeared calmer. I asked her how she was feeling, and she replied that she was feeling better. She reported a little tiff with her driver. He was angry with her for some small reason. Usually she would be insulted, but this time she paused, asked herself what she had to learn from this incident and held her tongue. She realized that she had to learn not to overreact. She had to let go of these small things. Minimize, don't maximize the small things in life. This was part of her lesson plan! I wish I had a picture of my face at that moment. I smiled broadly, gave my patient a high five and praised her. She had made a huge cognitive shift in how to behave in an upsetting moment. She had learned how to reframe anger and fear into a simple life lesson. Don't sweat the small stuff, let it go. She had learned a huge lesson! Her task now is to let go of the weird things that happen every Thursday as quickly as possible.

The Spirituality of Oneness is the goal. Life is God's plan for reaching it.

We can resist as long as we want. Time, as we think of it, doesn't even exist. However, eventually the lesson plan works.

Here are the Cliff Notes:

- Accept life as a lesson plan.
- Develop spiritual thoughts, feelings, behavior, values and insights.
- If you are having trouble with the above, "fake it until you make it."
- Ask for God's help through prayer, meditation and questioning your inner self.
- Let go of anger, fear and guilt
- Let go, let God
- Accept healing
- Life is a great cosmic lesson plan. Ask yourself: Is this a teachable moment?

It is an old adage that, "when the student is ready, the teacher appears!" It took the tragedy of 9/11 to arouse enough anxiety in me to find the writings of Dr. Thomas Hora. The next chapter is a piece I wrote shortly after 9/11.

CHAPTER 2

The Only Answer There Is

In the fall of 2001, a thought struck me like a thunderbolt. The increased anxiety and depression I had been experiencing since the September 11 attacks was only a worsening of my usual existential anxiety. My mind kept bouncing between fearing and hating the terrorists. Those bad guys were ruining my life. They had seemingly destroyed my secure and peaceful existence. Instead of waking up each day and doing what I liked, I had to think about anthrax, smallpox, bombing and maybe even an apocalypse. Everybody seemed to agree on my take of the events, except my mystical friends. They talked about forgiveness and purging of fears to reach a higher level of spirituality. According to them, I was supposed to be thankful to Bin Laden and his legation of evil cohorts for bringing me closer to enlightenment. I did not feel thankful. I did not need terrorists killing people to remind me that I will die...someday... "Wait a minute, I thought... perhaps I am in denial about death."

I began to inquire inwardly, seeking answers from my higher self. What part of me was afraid of dying? my ego? Yes, I was still too attached to my ego. I was still acting like an ego defending its body. Where did this ego come from? It developed through synthesizing emotional experiences in early childhood. At first, it was merely a body ego. Then, gradually, it moved up to my head and I began to develop a separate psychological identity. This newly formed ego told me that I was separate from everyone else, had to compete with everyone else and hopefully become a winner, a person with high self- esteem. I thought I was just an ego, encased in a body and would someday die…but not for a long time.

Fear of Extinction

My original psychological path was focused on analyzing the reasons why I wasn't more of a winner, more successful. As one early therapist of mine put it, "You always want to look good." I agreed with him that I wanted to look good. But doesn't everyone want to look good?" I didn't get his point. Under the surface, I felt I was "not good enough," so I wanted to appear to be a total winner. My therapist was telling me I had a compulsive need to "look good," so I could feel like a winner. This psychotherapy session took place in 1974 and at that time, spirituality had never entered the picture for me, or my therapist. I also suffered from existential anxiety but I considered that "normal." It was a fear of extinction that would someday come, but not for a long time.

During the 1980s, I encountered *A Course in Miracles*. It seemed to have some good ideas: *Come together in holy relationships. Forgive everyone, not because you are superior or more spiritual but because you are part of God. Pray to God or the Holy-Spirit to see things differently and create win-win interpretations in daily life. Only our perceptions are real. Healing our negative, perceptions of life is the only real healing. The body and the physical world are the illusions.* Whoa…wait a minute, were they telling me that the real world is an illusion, that pain isn't real? Were they were saying the real cause of all guilt and pain is "the separation" from God. Yes, that is what they were saying. This philosophy was too far out even for me at that time. I put the book down for ten years.

During the 1990s I studied many alternative philosophies of life. I embraced the concepts of reincarnation and Karma. I engaged in past life therapy, as a participant as well as a therapist. Past life therapy was helpful. Intellectually it made sense. Yet, with the terrorist attack of 9/11, I went back into massive fear of death.

Let us fast forward to 2001. During that year, I encountered the work of Dr. Thomas Hora, a New York psychiatrist who created existential psychiatry. Dr. Hora tells us that all suffering is caused by "self-confirmatory ideation." This sounded remarkably similar to *A Course in Miracles'* idea that we cause our own suffering with the illusion that we are separate from God. According to Dr. Hora, we are dreaming that the physical world is real and this illusion is causing us pain (especially those darn terrorists). To make things worse, we will go to almost any lengths to **confirm** that we are **nothing but** separate physical beings. As long as we refuse to look to Spirit for answers, says Dr. Hora, we remain trapped in pain and suffering. What about purely physical pain? Dr. Hora advises us that all pain is related to angry "interaction thoughts." Again, as in the Course, we see ourselves as completely separate from one another, and are angry at others for frustrating our desires. When we feel the resultant physical pain, most of us deny any connection to an angry thought. We would rather believe pain just happens. Personally, I can accept the connection between repressed anger and pain. This idea seems intuitively right to me. What then was the reason for my difficulty dealing with the anger at and fear of those terrorists? I needed someone to blame for my psychological and physical pain. My target was terrorists.

We Are Not Separate

Our need to see ourselves as purely physical and separate is deeply rooted in cultural belief. Many of us in this country have been raised to be scientific- materialists. For scientific materialists, it seems obvious that we are nothing but our bodies controlled by our conscious minds. The alternative idea of unity or oneness is difficult to comprehend. Both Dr. Hora and *A Course in Miracles* tell us that we are part of the "loving intelligence" that is God. I, along with everyone else need to **identify** my being with God, not my body and ego.

I have found that meditating helps my spiritual process along. Letting go of **all** thoughts and feelings non-judgmentally points us in the right direction. Allowing all our thoughts and feelings to arise *and be released* helps us too. The more allowing and releasing we do, the more we are able to get in touch with our **higher self, our soul**. At the soul level we know that we are one with God and all is well. There is no cause and effect, just love and peace. There is no suffering, only joy. We must be willing to engage in this spiritual awakening process by working with the physical and emotional being. Meditation helps us see beyond the physical separation between all beings. We must be willing to recognize that everything our common sense and cultural conditioning has taught us *is backwards*. We are not purely separate, physical beings generating consciousness. We are also, at a deeper level, consciousness, generating our physical beings. As long as we are trapped in separation and physicality, we cannot achieve real peace of mind. We are here to move toward enlightenment by *realizing* our true spiritual source.

CHAPTER 3

We Have Everything Backwards

M. Scott Peck wrote a book in the 1970s called *The Road Less Traveled.*
He expected to sell a few thousand copies. Instead, he sold a few
million copies and was number one on the *New York Times* best-
seller list for several years. The book was about our reluctance to face
ourselves and accept the reality that life is essentially spiritual. The
opening sentence of this book was, "Life is difficult." How sad but true.
Have you ever wondered why life is difficult for practically everyone?
Is it supposed to be that difficult? Is there any way to make it easier?
Is there any point to life at all? These are some of the questions Peck
was striving to answer.

At about the same time, Helen Shuckman was scribing *A Course in
Miracles.* This remarkable book went even farther out on the spiritual
limb than Peck. As we mentioned in chapter two, *The Course* says we are
here for one reason and one reason only, to wake up from the dream of
purely physical life. According to Dr. Ken Wapnick, one of Shuckman's
early collaborators, we can wake up quickly or slowly. Dr. Wapnick
recommends the slow awakening. He feels that if we wake up too quickly,
we might be in shock. In other words, it is easier to wake up from a "good"
dream than from a nightmare. As an experienced psychotherapist, I would
have to agree with Dr. Wapnick. People in the midst of a nightmarish
life need to find some stability in physical life before transcending it. I
have found cognitive therapy, reframing distressing events and creating

15

more positive beliefs about life helpful. This has been my experience with clients, as well as my personal experience.

I would like to share two personal stories. These events were turning points for me in the development of my psycho-spiritual outlook on life. The first took place twenty-five years ago. The other took place eleven years ago. Both events shattered my life and led to my gradual awakening from the dream of physical "reality."

Waking Up From My Dream

The first experience concerned a very difficult patient. This woman was successful in the world, but chronically depressed. We engaged in straight psychotherapy for several years with only slight improvement. She continued to drink heavily and was often depressed. She also began an intense "love" affair, but claimed he could not marry the (very unstable) man. Finally, she broke up with him and felt a little better until he called him to say that he was impulsively marrying someone else and moving far away. She fell apart completely at this news, feeling she had made a major mistake. She was hospitalized for depression and eventually released. However, she remained trapped in his nightmare. I tried every which way to help, including some spiritual guidance, which she claimed was "bullshit." He was determined to stay in his self-imposed ego-directed suffering. She needed someone to blame, however, and this someone was me! She decided that I had ruined her life with my therapy, She especially disliked the spirituality I was trying to introduce to her. She came in for daily therapy though, and barraged me with phone calls in between sessions. She was desperately looking for support, yet, rejecting any answers I could lead him to.

I became increasingly depressed. A psychic told me that this patient had killed me in a previous life. So I did a past life regression to release the karma. The regression confirmed the psychic's opinion. I experienced myself as a Jew in Roman times. I experienced my patient as a Roman soldier, on horseback. He jumped off his horse and killed me by choking me. It was an interesting experience, under hypnosis, but didn't help the situation. My therapist, who at first seemed helpful, turned out to be an alcoholic and showed up drunk to a session. Thus, I quit therapy and became despondent. I sought supervision from another psychologist, but there was still no relief. Finally, it occurred to me that no *person* could help me. Only God could help me. So I began to pray earnestly for the first time in my life. I prayed to be released from the painful situation. I kept hearing an inner voice say, "It will end soon, in an unusual way."

Soon after that, during a session, my patient stood up and announced, "You have ruined my life, now I am going to kill you."

She lunged at me, knocking me off my chair and started to choke me. Surprisingly, my inner voice guided me not to hit her but to shout, "Calm down, calm down." She did and we talked. This all occurred on the eve of Passover, the Jewish holiday of freedom from slavery. She did let go, as did I. We were both released, free. God had answered my prayers, in an unusual way. My ego couldn't solve the problem, but when I turned it over and prayed for guidance, I was released. About a year later we met on the street, on Christmas Eve. We wished each other well and parted in peace and forgiveness. I felt some sense of closure and dedicated myself to integrating prayer into a spiritual psychotherapy. My first book was written soon after, *When Therapy Isn't Enough: The Healing Power of Prayer and Psychotherapy.*

The Power of the Ego

From 1989 when this incident occurred, until 2002, I made slow but steady progress integrating spirituality into psychotherapy. For a long time, I put *A Course in Miracles* aside. I intuitively knew that it contained major wisdom, but I just couldn't get over some of the Course theology. I embraced the concept of forgiveness but had trouble with the reason for it. The Course says, "What does it mean to forgive because nothing really happened?" I loved the idea of forgiveness as part of atonement but didn't feel "at one" with everyone. I prayed daily for friends, family and myself. But I was too focused on physical health and healing. I knew the only real healing was psychological but I, along with most others, just wanted to feel good. It is tough to buck your conditioning and an entire culture based on material wealth and comfort. Still, I thought I was making some progress at spiritual growth. That is until November 4, 2002, when I had a heart attack.

I had been having difficulty breathing for a couple of days but made no connection to my heart. After all, I had none of the risk factors for heart disease. Yet, as I arrived at my office on November 4, my condition worsened and I asked my friend, healer Marcy Prisco to call 9-1-1. I was taken to the ER. The last thing I remember was talking to the doctor. Then, my consciousness changed. Everyone was running around and things seemed to be in slow motion. I was hit twice by a defibrillator and screamed loudly in agony. I awakened the next day in another hospital to find out I had almost died the day before. I had no typical "near death" experience, only a blank space and a buzzing noise. My wife told me she had gathered several friends who had prayed for me in the waiting room. Word spread and soon, many people were praying for my recovery. The doctors told my wife I might die that night.

Obviously, I lived. As far as I am concerned, the prayer, as well as the expert doctor, had saved my life. After a week hospital stay, I returned home to recover. I was in complete, abject fear of death. No amount of prayer, meditation, spiritual healing or anything else helped. I would get in bed at night and physically tremble. The doctors medicated me to the hilt with Plavix, Mavix, Toprol, aspirin, tranquilizers and mood elevators. I took vitamins and supplements galore. I had two more surgical procedures in a year to open blockages caused by scar tissue. I engaged in "thought field therapy" to release the trauma and traditional psychotherapy to soothe my soul, but nothing really helped much. I had to help myself by releasing my ego and turning to the Higher Power. Only the Higher Power could release me from the twin troubles of materialism and narcissism.

My ego, of course, advised me to seek constant help and advice from a multitude of people. I am using the term "ego" here in a spiritual sense. The way I am using it combines the Freudian notion of id, ego and superego. The id ego, superego system keeps us focused on life as a separate individual with conflicting goals. The id is pure pleasure seeking. It wants what it wants, aggressively and sexually. The superego is a learned set of rules to control the powerful id impulses. This "inner war" is mediated by the psychological ego. Due to this inner war, we rarely focus on the higher self or soul, which is connected to God. What I really needed to do, at that time, was to turn to the Higher Self and pray for guidance. The ego asked for a miracle cure to heal the body, the mind would come around later. I needed to release all ego goals first and turn my life over to the Higher Self. The ego always wants to preserve itself at all costs. It urged me to forget the spiritual stuff e.g. higher self, mind and just cure the body so it could go on in the usual manner. Did spirituality bring me inner peace in 2003? No. But through that experience, I did deeply understand that my ego was and is indeed the enemy of peace.

Turning to Spirit

Gradually, I turned to Spirit and ignored ego. In fact, now, whatever my ego says, I do what George Costanza did on the TV show *Seinfeld* — the opposite. If the ego tells me to work harder, I ease up. If the ego tells me I am not good enough, I tell myself I am good enough, right now. If the ego tells me I just have to suffer with physical symptoms the rest of my life, I turn the symptoms over to God and affirm that I will be comfortable again. If the ego tells me I am going to die any minute, I turn my life over to God again, asking only to live long enough to complete my life plan.

The life plan is to embrace the "spiritual cognitive shift", to see life as a lesson in forgiveness, kindness, love and peace. I know part of my plan is to share this spiritual shift with as many others as possible. I have been given many gifts and I intend to use them as long as I am here. Despite the pull of the ego (narcissism) and the body (materialism), I now know that I am an emanation of the Holy Spirit. We are all individualized aspects of God, in the process of waking up from the dream of physical "reality" to the reality of our life in the heavenly spiritual world. My friends, we have everything backwards. By turning to Spirit for guidance and help we can regain Spiritual reality and imagine along with John Lennon that we can "live as one."

The Final Word

So let's assume there is a" great cosmic lesson plan." What is it that keeps more of us from getting on board and learning what needs to be learned? If I had to boil it down to one word, the word would be "guilt." That may seem to be a strange choice. However, the next two chapters clearly show why I choose guilt as public enemy number one! The other contenders were fear and anger. However, from my vantage point, primal guilt (sometimes called shame or unworthiness of being happy) is always lurking beneath the surface. The next two chapters articulate this point of view. We must heal the vicious circle of guilt, anger and fear if we hope to heal ourselves and ultimately the planet!

CHAPTER 4

Guilty? Me?

There are three basic emotions that may block healing: fear, anger and guilt. I have chosen guilt, the most hidden emotion of the big three, as my starting point for this chapter. Our unconscious acceptance of guilt (shame) in early childhood leads to much unnecessary suffering, sometimes called, "the human condition." A young child feels like he or she is the center of the world. If anything happens in early childhood, the child feels as if it's her fault. This normal narcissism of early childhood is part of the developmental process we all go through. Theoretically, if everyone around us in childhood were happy and cheerful all the time, we would also be very happy. Unfortunately, few people are raised in such ideal families. Thus, the normal narcissism of early childhood leads us to hang on to the idea that we are responsible for everything that happens around us. But for most of us, this idea never goes away. In other words, we are fixated at an early childhood way of thinking and feeling about ourselves. Even as adults, we believe that it is somehow our fault that the people around us are unhappy.

As the self-centeredness of early childhood fades, the guilt gets automatically repressed into the unconscious mind. The catch is that it is still there, creating pain, suffering and feelings of unworthiness. Some people accept this guilt and unworthiness. They develop an unconscious belief in guilt which is then manifested in negative events, feelings of inadequacy and a need to be punished. Other people deny any guilt or responsibility for negative events or feelings. Instead, they get angry at others (the guilty ones), and blame them for anything that goes wrong. If there is nobody in the vicinity to blame, there is always the government, big business, life itself or even God to blame for anything that goes wrong. The "guilties" think they need to be punished. Other people are unhappy and it is their fault. The "angries" are in denial of their painful guilty feelings. Thus, they project them on the "guilty" people around them. The "angries" are more than willing to criticize or yell at the "guilties." This is often found in marriage.

The third emotion (of the big three) is fear. The "guilties" fear that they will never get what they want. They think that all they will get is more punishment. The "angries" fear retribution for their wrath. So everyone has fear. Anxiety is probably the number one complaint people bring to my office. The other big issue people have is depression. Depression is, according to psychoanalytic theory, anger turned inward. This is true, but it is also related to guilt. We are depressed because we think we don't deserve to be happy. The hidden belief in unworthiness plus guilt and internalized anger often manifests as depression. There is a vicious circle of negative emotions that seems to be part of the human condition. Guilt leads to anger which leads to fear. The vicious circle continues, suffering continues and nobody realizes that there is a way out. I believe that the biological aspects of depression arise as a result of long standing negative emotions and beliefs. I think it is exactly the opposite of what modern psychiatry thinks.

A Way Out

The way out of the vicious circle is awareness. As Sigmund Freud recommended, make the unconscious conscious. However, just making it conscious does not necessarily release the toxic emotions. The twelve step traditions go a step further. They recommend letting go and turning the emotions over to a higher power: "Let go, let God!" In other words, it is Spirit or God that enables us to let go of control. But, according to the founder of existential metapsychiatry, Dr. Thomas Hora, there is a third step: to accept healing. Dr. Hora said, "**God helps those who let him.**" God is the higher power, pure energy, pure love, the ground of being, our source. Accepting healing means letting go of the perfect control we all want from our conscious, ego level of being. The ego is a belief system. It is the result of a synthesis of all of our experiences. This belief system (ego) is glued together by the guilt, anger and fear. The ego part of us believes it is all we are. Thus, it is terrified of change. It does not want to change, despite the suffering. The ego's answer to suffering is more control, through more will power. However, if we become willing to let go of the toxic emotions, Spirit takes over, allowing the "egoic" negative beliefs to change.

We can identify instead, with positive, spiritual beliefs. Dr. Hora recommends peace, assurance, gratitude and love (PAGL). This is the true healing! Releasing the guilt, anger and fear is the emotional healing (letting go).Turning to spirit instead of the ego (let go, let God) and allowing the beliefs to become spiritual is the real healing. I have purposely placed bodily healing last. It is usually placed first. (As we know by now, we have everything backwards. The body (the densest layer of our being) may be healed as part of the spiritual-psychological process but the culprit in all bodily suffering is stress (actually distress). The emotional distress creates stress hormones, like high cortisol, which then destroy cells and organs. To recap, the distress comes from listening to the ego while ignoring or denying spirit. The release of the toxic emotions opens us up to Spirit instead of ego (allow healing). As Spirit is allowed to be in charge, healing on all levels, including the mind and body, can take place. The emotional, cognitive and spiritual healings described in this chapter lead to relaxation and cellular, organic and bodily healing.

Let me recap: The blockages to healing are the stressful circle of guilt, anger and fear. The healing requires three steps, Let go, let God and accept healing. I sometimes use an acronym so patients can remember the three steps, LG, LGLG, AH! Say the acronym out loud and start feeling relief now! Several of my patients have used this system, especialy the acronym. The funny sound makes them laugh and that helps them let go.

In the next chapter, we'll take a deeper look at how guilt ruins our lives, and I'll recommend further techniques to release the guilt underlying human suffering and unhappiness.

CHAPTER 5

Guilt, Anger and the Human Condition

Are you a guilty person? Are you bothered by a nagging feeling that something is wrong with your life? Do angry people seem to choose you as their target for no good reason? Do you keep yourself very busy so you won't have to think about yourself too much?

If you answered yes to any of these questions, read on. If you answered "no" to all of them, you are either a very happy person...or you are in denial. Probably you are in denial. So read on anyway. You might discover that you have some inner guilt. After all, most guilt is unconscious. It is just too painful to feel the brunt of our guilt.

The Pain of Denial

As we discussed in the previous chapter, psychologists since the time of Sigmund Freud have been trying to educate us about the ways in which we protect ourselves from feeling the pain of guilt. The number one defense mechanism on the hit parade is denial. Young children often deny doing things they just did, right in front of you. Even when confronted by adults they deny it. Only with maturity do people begin to admit what they have done. With even greater maturity they learn to accept the consequences of what they have done. This does not usually occur until adolescence, maybe later, and sometimes never. There are those who never admit responsibility for anything. Schizophrenics, criminals, alcohol and drug abusers, narcissists, all deny responsibility for their actions. The fear of the consequences of their actions is too great. To feel guilty is to think you did something wrong. In a court of law, guilt requires punishment. Life is like a court of law. If you think you are guilty, you will find some way to get punished for it. Most of the time the punishment comes in the form of other people, or life in general, giving you problems, situations and feelings you don't want.

If you are completely unaware of your own guilt and need for punishment, you will see no connection when the troubling person or situation gives you a hard time. For example, you may be criticized harshly by a spouse or boss. You react with righteous indignation or anger. "How dare he attack me! I didn't do anything wrong. I am angry and going to stay angry until he apologizes." You may rant and rave, or turn it inward and get depressed, or develop a physical condition like a headache, stomach ache or worse. You may also develop anxiety out of fear of retribution for my retaliatory anger. It is a vicious circle. The tragedy of it all is that neither party realizes that the whole conflict has to do with unconscious guilt and self-hate. The one who is more aware of the guilt, sometimes called a depressive (or victim, loser, schlemiel) attracts another person with unconscious guilt. This person is so unconscious that they prefer to project out their guilt onto someone else. The angry person proclaims, "It isn't my fault…it is your fault." This is projection, another attempt to remain unaware of guilt and self-hate. The ball is now in the depressive's court. She might respond by counter attacking, getting more depressed, or getting sicker in some way. The vicious circle may spiral out of control, with all parties feeling misunderstood, victimized and unhappy. *This is the dynamic behind all human conflict.* It leads to the entire range of human misery, depression, anxiety, divorce, illness, and on a global scale war. All of it is caused by one simple human emotion.….

GUILT!

What Your Parents Have to Do with Your Guilt

Guilt is an emotional discomfort that arises when we feel we have not lived up to some responsibility or have done something wrong. It doesn't mean we actually *did* do something wrong, we just have to *think* we did something wrong, to paraphrase the great philosopher Rene Descartes, I think I am guilty, therefore I am guilty. This is an important distinction. Now if you think you did something wrong, you have to be punished, somehow, *and you will find a way*. Now why do so many, if not all of us, think we did something wrong? There are two levels to be explored, the psychological and the spiritual.

Psychological guilt develops as we are born into and adapt to the physical world. Psychologists call this process "separation-individuation." This term means that in order to survive in the physical world, we need to gradually realize that we are separate individuals. We need to identify with our bodies, realize we are physically separate from mother and learn how to deal with and cope with all the other seemingly separate individuals in this world of "blooming, buzzing confusion" (William James.) This is usually called developing a healthy ego. Under ideal conditions, our caretakers show us warmth, love and compassion. They guide us through all the difficulties of toddlerhood and early childhood. They give us appropriate limits at each age and enforce the rules consistently. They never use guilt or fear to control us. We grow up to be happy, healthy, young adults with high self-esteem and great caring for others. Will all those who were raised this way please raise their hand? I never met anyone who was raised like that!

Now, what about the rest of us? Many of us were raised by immature and inconsistent parents with plenty of their own insecurities and issues. They tried their best, but were often overwhelmed by the process of making a living and raising a family. They tried to love us and set limits, but did it inconsistently. Maybe one parent drank too much, or took drugs. They used fear and guilt to control us far too often, just as their parents did with them. They just didn't know any better. Sometimes they treated us with outright abuse or neglect. The result is that we were traumatized. Each time we were yelled at or hit or told that we weren't good enough, we took it to heart. The nature of children, is that they think the world revolves around them. If they are being mistreated, they think they deserved it. What do you think the result is? You guessed it...

GUILT!

(The following is a parody of the introduction to the old 1950s Superman TV show)

"More powerful than a locomotive - able to destroy whole populations like an epidemic - look... out at the world....It's an ache, it's a pain...no it's GUILT...

Yes, its guilt, strange emotion from another planet with power and ability to destroy mortal man...guilt, who is disguised in every man, destroying all who feel it or deny it, suffer with fear anger, and the physical way."

Seriously now, it is almost impossible to grow up without trauma, guilt and fear. Parenting is a very difficult job and most people stink at it because of their own problems. Most parents, however, are in denial that they stink at parenting. Consequently, the kids feel guilty because the parents tell them to be guilty (without realizing it.) Parental blaming, plus the normal narcissistic nature of childhood, equals a very guilty populace. Am I blaming the parents? Actually no! This is just the way it is. And human life is difficult because of the way it is set up. Most of us grow up in the competitive world of school and work, trying to prove that we are good enough, while "knowing" inside that we are not good enough (because of guilt and unworthiness).

Guilt is the Human Condition

Now, this is much too painful for most folks to bear. They have to deny their guilt, pretend it doesn't exist, and blame someone else. This is done by the previously mentioned defense mechanisms of denial and projection. I must, at this point, add in the granddaddy of all defenses — repression. This is the *automatic* pushing of pain into the unconscious. So we can be very guilty and not even know about it. *The end result of all this inner guilt and turmoil in the outer world is fear, hate and conflict.* Guilt is the source of all human conflict. I have just outlined the psychological reasons for guilt. Yet, that does not go deep enough. We must also explore the spiritual basis for guilt.

The spiritual basis for guilt is a feeling of separation from God (the Infinite, our Source). Our materialistic western culture would have us believe that we are nothing but biological creatures, with an ego to guide us through life, after which we are obliterated. This is the paradigm many of us were taught. Some of us were taught about God in religious school. We were taught that God knows all about us, if we are bad, we will be punished. If guilt is the root of all suffering, and there is some spiritual basis for guilt, let us root it out and heal it. The big point is....

A Feeling of Separation from God Causes All Suffering!!!

Therefore, healing the split with God is the central task for healing each person's pain. Indeed, it is the central task for healing the persistent conflict between individuals and nations.

We must stop projecting God out as a separate being who is punishing us for our guilt (like our parents on the psychological level). The ultimate answer for humanity is to wake up and realize that, on the spiritual level, we are one with God. That is to say, we are emanations of All That Is - our Source - God. This concept comes from Kabbalistic Judaism, as well as Buddhism and Eastern religions. God's nature is love, peace and power. Thus, our nature is love, peace and power. But, since we are alienated and think we are separate from God, we feel instead, guilt, fear and anger on a regular basis.

An Outline for Releasing Guilt

To release guilt, first, we must admit our underlying guilt and heal this emotion. Second, we must heal our relationship with God, and develop our spirituality. Spiritually-oriented psychotherapy can help. It involves releasing your feelings of separation from others (true forgiveness) and God. Meditation and prayer are invaluable tools in the process. They help us to promote spiritual values. We need to learn to release the negative emotions and beliefs caused by guilt. As we make progress in letting go of negative emotions, we will develop forgiveness and compassion for others.

There are several methods that can be used to release guilt, either as part of spiritual psychotherapy or on your own. The first is prayer/meditation. The second is the "Sedona Method."

Four Types of Prayer

There are basically four types of prayer explained by Aldous Huxley in his remarkable book, *The Perennial Philosophy.* They are: petition, intercession, adoration and contemplation. All can be used to heal guilt. Petition involves speaking to God and asking for something. Usually people ask for magical healing of symptoms, money or a love object. In this case, we are not asking for such externals. Instead we are asking for relief from guilt. One form the prayer might take would be, "Please God, release me from guilt feelings." An even better prayer would be "Thank you God for releasing me from guilt feelings and all subsequent results of that guilt. A still better prayer might be, "I am released from all guilt feelings, now! Thank you God." This last prayer implies that God is both immanent and transcendent, within and without you. It assumes that the goal has already been reached and is now being affirmed and actualized.

The second form of prayer is intercession. That is, praying for someone else. It is best to get permission from the person. It is possible to pray for someone without permission, but it is better to get permission. It shows that they really want to get well.

The third form of prayer is adoration. That is, we affirm the greatness, lovingness and power of God to heal all problems. Such a prayer might be, "Thank you all powerful and loving God for proceeding with my healing on all levels — spiritual, psychological and physical. I am healing through faith and trust in your grace."

The fourth type of prayer is contemplation or meditation. With this type of prayer, "being" is stressed over action. For example, in Buddhist insight meditation, one just sits and follows the breath. What occurs next is that thoughts and feelings will emerge. The inner observer just watches and waits. No matter what the thoughts are, we sit and observe them objectively. We do not push them away, we simply observe them as they come and go. Each time we have a distracting thought we go back to the breath and connect to the life force within. The same process is followed when feelings or sensations emerge. We just watch, dispassionately and go back to the breath. After a while, we realize that all psychological and physical phenomena are just temporary distractions from ultimate reality, which is spirit, manifesting in physical human form. The final goal is peace and enlightenment.

The Sedona Method

Another way of releasing guilt is the "Sedona Method" invented by Lester Levenson, and popularized by Hale Dwoskin and Larry Crane. Lester Levenson was a hard driving, successful businessman in the 1950s. He suddenly developed heart problems. He had a heart attack and was told to do as little as possible. He realized that his emotions were ruining his physical health. As he struggled with his fate, he developed a method of self-questioning that he eventually called "The Sedona Method." In a similar fashion to meditation, he would ask himself if he could release whatever emotion he was feeling. The questions were simple. Could I release this emotion? Would I release it? If so, when could I release it? It can be shortened to could ya? would ya? when? You may then visualize the emotion (guilt) releasing. Or you may feel it releasing by itself. Or, you may dive into the feeling, letting it come up in its intensity and then release. The more guilt (as well as anger and fear) you release, the more peaceful, happy, successful and loving you become. For me, the Sedona Method is also a prayerful method. It is like questioning our inner spiritual source. This inner teacher might also be thought of as the immanent God.

It is important to note at this juncture that releasing guilt is more than just a technique to magically cure yourself or anyone else. We must also look for the lesson and meaning in each life event. The human tendency is to try to pray away all problems and sail through life easily and happily. If that doesn't occur, we begin to doubt the efficacy of prayer and the power of God. That is because of our misunderstanding about what prayer is and how God answers prayer. God simply has a different agenda or lesson plan.

To God, prayer is not a simple technique to get rid of suffering. Rather, it is an alignment of our values with spiritual values. Every time we have a problem, we need to align ourselves with God or Spirit better. If there is no spiritual learning, or "repentance" (rethinking), there may not be any change on the physical or psychological level - thus, the answer has been given. The answer is *No*. We haven't let go of the guilt, anger or fear yet, so we don't get healed yet. "Keep trying," God replies, "I will give you strength." Keep praying and the answer will be changed when we are healed *spiritually*. Remember, we are spiritual beings first and foremost. Changing physical phenomena is just an arena for spiritual learning.

The ultimate goal is a sense of oneness with the source, God. In more pragmatic terms this would mean feelings of happiness, joy, even bliss — not all the time, but whenever we are properly aligned. Behaviorally, we would be kinder, gentler and more peaceful in our relationships with others. There is tremendous pull by our physical and ego selves to move away from spirituality and toward the pleasures of sensory gratification. We need to gradually move away from spending all of our time gratifying the senses and spend more time in contemplation of the spiritual side of ourselves. Spiritual therapy, prayer and meditation will, over time, show us what we really are, spiritual beings, on a human adventure.

It is time to let go of our hidden inner guilt, let it go and develop our spiritual side.

It is our only chance for real happiness.

The fate of humanity awaits our collective decision.

On Anger

But what about anger? It is always lurking in our unconscious mind. Guilt feels bad. It is a large part of depression. We often reach a point where we are tired of blaming ourselves for everything. The most common way to get rid of that guilty feeling is to get angry and find somebody or some group to attack. Husbands attack wives. Wives attack husbands. Republicans attack Democrats. Democrats attack Republicans. And so on, and so on.

You see, the truth of the matter is, ***anger is more fun than guilt.*...**

If it seems that I am obsessed by the concept of guilt, I must confess that I did have a Jewish mother, who constantly reminded me that, "Nobody ever helps me around here." (Anne Menahem 1919-2011.). However, my training in psychodynamics helped a lot too! *A Course in Miracles* emphasizes psychodynamics as well as metaphysics. When I teach my graduate students at Teachers College, Columbia University about the Course, I always emphasize the psychodynamics first. It makes a lot of sense for therapists to help their patients let go of guilt, anger and fear. The peaceful Oneness feelings will inevitably emerge. Releasing guilt, anger and fear is the meeting place for psychology and spirituality. This is a daunting task for each of us. We must let go of negative emotions and change our beliefs. In order to do this we must change our priorities. Consistent with the already mentioned work of Dr. Thomas Hora, as well as, Judeo-Christian thought, we must shift from material values to spiritual values. We'll delve into this concept in the next chapter.

CHAPTER 6

What Does God Want From Us?

Let's begin the exploration of what God might want from us with some simple premises:

Premise Number One:

There is a God, a higher power, transcending human beings, yet, inherent in each human being. This God is creative, loving, and intelligent. This God is one with all that is, visible and invisible. Thus, this God is all knowing and all powerful.

Premise Number Two:

Human beings are much more than we think we are, more than just separate bodies, doomed to extinction at death. In reality, we humans have our being within the One God. We are emanations, in material form, of the One God. Just because we can't always see or sense our spiritual essence, does not mean it isn't real. It is more real than our obvious physical selves.

Premise Number Three:

All worldly and human problems stem from our lack of awareness of God. All disease, suffering, famine, pestilence, wars, atrocities and violence are ultimately results of our lack of God awareness. Most people spend most of their time focused on physical survival, physical pleasure and ego gratification. Much less time is spent in pursuit of God or spiritual values. If existence is perceived as separate from God or worse yet, if there is no awareness of God at all, it would take a very mature person to forgo individual gain for the common good. Most people are much too self-centered and narcissistic for this to happen. However, in my mind, there is a God, who wants something from us. Understanding what God wants, and why God wants it is the key to the transformation of the human race.

So what does God want from us?

God simply wants us to be fully cognizant, aware and understanding of what we really are and what He really is. This awareness of our oneness with God will make our lives meaningful, manageable and merciful.

That's it? That's all? Is that the big deal? So what? How does that help end disease, war, famine? How does it help us cope with suffering and death?

I believe full awareness and understanding of our Godly, spiritual nature will inevitably lead to the eradication of all human problems. If all individuals understood God and felt peaceful, loving, and kind, they would naturally help their brothers and sisters in any way possible. Each person, fully understanding and seeing the Godly nature of the Self would naturally want to help others. We would love our neighbors as ourselves because all others would be seen as the same as us, individually expressing their divine nature in a human, embodied way. It would be clearly evident that spiritual values such as forgiveness, kindness, peacefulness and cooperation are the only way to go. There would be no war. There would be no violence. There would be no stress, leading to disease. There would be no fear, for all fear is related to physical or psychological harm.

How Do We Get There?

So, now we know what does God wants from us. How do we get there? First, God wants us to be good people, who love ourselves as well as our fellow human beings. The requirement is to find a way that works for us to experience and embrace Godly values. A full understanding and experiencing that we are indeed one with the One God would naturally lead to peace, harmony, health and well-being for humans.

If you are with me so far, you might have a few objections. I can hear my detractors now. The objection might go something like this:

"That is fine, theoretically, but what about evil people? What about war? What about terrible diseases? What about starvation? How can God awareness eliminate these very physical and psychological problems?"

The answer is that each person who has a glimmer of spiritual yearning must get on a spiritual path. Meditation, prayer and or a spiritual practice are essential. The transformation needs to be manifest on all levels. Thoughts, feelings and behaviors need transformation. There needs to be a spiritual-cognitive shift. First, this shift will occur in a few striving persons. Then, it could spread to whole groups. Eventually, the shift could be the majority. This has been called the "tipping point" for the human race. In a world where most people think, feel and behave according to spiritual values like peace, love, kindness and forgiveness, the minority would soon be transformed or die out due to natural selection.

Beware of any group that has the only answer, the only path to salvation or the only true name for God. There is only one God no matter what the name. Thus, it is the inner experience of the transcendent and immanent God that leads to the "revolution" of consciousness.

God wants us to work on ourselves to develop the understanding and experience of our spiritual nature. Then (and only then), can there be a happy, peaceful world.

Get started! Here are a few ways:

- Pray for help with this immense journey.
- Meditate on the Godly, Buddha nature (spiritual source).
- Forgive others, recognizing, that you are really, at a deep level, one with them in God.

- Experience the peace, happiness and joy of understanding your spiritual nature.
- Live your life according to inner, spiritual knowing and spiritual values.
- Perform random acts of loving-kindness.

Only good will follow from these loving thoughts, feelings and behaviors.

CHAPTER 7

Forgiveness: The Key to Successful Psychotherapy

Now that we've discussed what God wants from us, let's examine in more detail the concept of forgiveness. Forgiveness is the key to successful psychotherapy. Most people in psychotherapy have interpersonal problems and /or intra-psychic problems related to handling inevitable fear, anger and guilt. In the kind of spiritual psychotherapy that I do, I've found that utilizing a combination of cognitive methods, meditation, prayer and spiritual insight has proven to be very effective in easing symptoms and facilitating positive character change.

A Jewish Perspective on Forgiveness

The story of Joseph and his brothers can give us a clue to how forgiveness heals guilt and anger. It seems that Joseph's jealous bothers had left him in a pit to die in the wilderness. Later, Joseph escaped the pit and became a noble in Egypt. The starving brothers come to Joseph with great fear and guilt, asking for food and forgiveness. They even offer to be his slaves. Joseph replies that he will not judge them harshly. He says that even though they tried to harm him, it was part of his Godly great lesson plan. The intended evil deed of leaving him in a pit eventually put Joseph in a position to help many people survive. So Joseph forgave his brothers. The brothers remained in Egypt and Joseph lived a good life, for 110 years.

Buddhist Perspectives on Forgiveness

Buddhist meditation practices, concentrative meditation, and petitionary prayers of thankfulness have also played a positive role in fostering positive personality change. The goal, as mentioned in the previous chapter is a spiritual-cognitive shift, away from blaming others or oneself for stress, anxiety and discomfort toward a new world view, similar to the Buddhist view of the universe, where the outer world is viewed as a lucid waking dream. Coping better with the world is facilitated by getting in touch with the Godly Buddha nature and experiencing profound release into a spiritual loving awareness. Instead of blaming others, awareness of Oneness, love and peace facilitate compassion and forgiveness for others and oneself.

Dealing with Resistance

There is an old story of a patient with extreme depression and anxiety. The patient implores the therapist to help him feel better. "I'll do anything," says the patient. The therapist says, "Just do this!" The patient replies, "anything but that!" This is, of course, known, resistance. In my forty years as a psychotherapist, I have found that the thing that patients resist the most is forgiveness! This is intriguing, since I have come to believe that the development of compassion and forgiveness is the key to successful psychotherapy and healing. Why then is there such resistance to such a simple solution to suffering? The answer, I believe, lies in developmental psychology. As detailed in my book, *When Therapy Isn't Enough* (Menahem, 1995), our human difficulties arise inevitably as we move from the oneness of the intrauterine state, to the separation from the mother and total dependency on her for food, warmth and nurturing. Even if we have what Dr. Melanie Klein described as, a "good enough" mother, there will be times when the food doesn't come fast enough or the nurturance to our discomfort is not immediately taken care of. These problems are inevitable.

Gradually through the first few years of life, the infant realizes that she is a separate creature. This is both good and bad. It is good in that we all have to learn to become independent and take care of ourselves eventually. It is bad because we now have to develop methods to get what we want, when we want or need it. The world now becomes a place that must be manipulated to get needs met. Again, this is very different from the oneness of intrauterine life. At each stage of separation-individuation there are challenges to be met in order to mature emotionally and negotiate the world. Healthy psychological development requires stable caregivers who skillfully adjust to the growing child and provide loving and consistent care and limits. My observation is that this almost never occurs.

The caregivers have their own human moods and are often inconsistent, angry, moody and unstable. This leads to what transpersonal theorist Ken Wilber calls "developmental lesions." This is Wilber's term for childhood traumas. The earlier the trauma, the worse the developmental arrest. For example, borderline, unstable personalities are the result of traumas at ages 2-3. As every therapist knows, "borderlines" are unstable and angry. They often project their anger on others, especially inconsistent caregivers or their substitutes. Eventually, grudges build up and persist. Is such an individual likely to let go of the anger and forgive the inconsistent, sometimes abusive caregiver, probably not? But the difficulty in letting go of anger is not limited to patients with borderline pathologies. Other, less troubled patients have the same resistance to forgiveness!

Resistance to forgiveness also occurs in my patients with more mature, "neurotic" fixations. For example, obsessive-compulsive patients are known for being very stubborn and holding on to the obsessional way of life. The obsessional thinking or compulsive behavior hides the angry refusal to do what the other person wants. Rather than becoming aware of the anger and guilt behind the symptom, the patient unconsciously chooses to hold on. How could such a person agree to forgive anyone? There seems to be nothing to forgive. They think they will just keep doing the compulsion and everything will work out? right? wrong! As mentioned in earlier chapters, the only way to heal is to become aware of emotions, let go of anger, fear and guilt and move toward forgiveness! Even if the patient does become aware of negative emotions, there is often a tendency to say, "Why should I forgive him? He hurt me. He is wrong and I am right. Let him apologize, then, maybe I'll let go of my grudge!"

Another common form of resistance to forgiveness is the alleged inability to do it. If anger, guilt or fear is acknowledged as a problem, the patient feels helpless to actually let go of the emotion! Patients often say, "But Doctor, how do I let it go and forgive?" This is actually a positive movement. The person is now aware of the problem and just does not know how to let go of it. It is an excellent opening for the introduction of meditation, affirmative prayer and cognitive therapy techniques.

The Path to Buddha Nature

As mentioned in earlier chapters, therapy can focus on letting go of the anger, facilitating the cognitive-emotional transformation that releases the patient toward achieving happiness and peace. I see therapy as a cognitive/spiritual process, with forgiveness as a central issue and technique. No matter what the level of developmental arrest, forgiveness is being resisted. As soon as forgiveness is embraced, negative beliefs can be replaced by positive ones. This leads to a better life. Eventually, there is a cognitive/spiritual embracing of the one true source, called the "Buddha nature" in Buddhism or God in Western religions.

Buddhists embrace the four noble truths of the Buddha. 1. All life is suffering. 2. Suffering is caused by clinging and desire. 3. Clinging and desire can be eliminated. 4. The path to enlightenment can be reached by following the eightfold path of the Buddha, which will be explained in the clinical example. The idea is that by following these guidelines, our values change. We will then be pursuing spiritual values, not strictly material values. For example, we will value cooperation over competition, peace over material possessions.

Our Buddha Nature

Meditation is the key to the whole process. Meditation puts us in touch with our Buddha nature. The result is a feeling of well-being, compassion for all sentient beings and thus forgiveness for the alleged "misdeeds" for which we are angry. There is no such thing as failure in meditation. Buddhists instruct us to "just sit" in meditation and the "results" will follow. I have found that meditation, combined with cognitive therapy, eventually results in a spiritual transcendence of attachment to anger. Cognitive therapy helps people change negative beliefs into positive ones.

For example, a deeply rooted, core belief that the world is against you will lead to anger, negative events and a perception of a hostile environment. The dissolution of this angry "glue" holding negative beliefs in place opens the door to "cognitive shifts" and more positive, spiritual beliefs. As the belief system improves, more and more positive things happen. When negative things happen, they are simply reframed in terms of the newer spiritual values. Each reframe makes it easier to cope with life. In that sense, therapy is palliative. It eases depression, anxiety and stress.

Eventually, the combination of cognitive therapy and meditation may result in transformation. According to Wilber, that means we look at life through an entirely different lens than we did before meditation and therapy started. Life is seen as a lucid dream from which we must "wake up" and perceive that reality is really our connectedness to each other and spirituality. We automatically interact with others from the point of view of the new more peaceful, loving reality, the Buddha nature. If this seems a little abstract, a case study may elucidate the point.

Larry's Story

When Larry started therapy, he was a 60-year-old history teacher. He suffered from extreme mood swings between depression and anger. His diagnosis was bipolar disorder. He had suffered through many deep depressions in which he was suicidal. At times he would come to sessions enraged at the behavior of his wife or his colleagues at work. He loved his work and students, but he was usually unhappy. Though he loved his two children, he felt his wife had often misunderstood him. He had waited a long time, until his mid–thirties, to get married and found that it did not cure his problems.

One day, he came in enraged at everything in his life, stating that he was going to kill himself or somebody else. A long calming session ensued. He refused to go to a hospital, but I called his wife and his psychiatrist. He made a medication appointment for the next day and promised to comply with the psychiatrist. He calmed down and promised to go home and not to do any harm to anyone. He followed through and gradually felt better. His doctor tried several medications and the crisis passed. Yet, clearly he needed more than medication to really heal. Therapy also seemed to help him-but only temporarily. Mostly, he derived benefit from learning how to reframe his life in a more light-hearted way. He liked situation comedies, so we would talk about how certain characters might be incorporated into his way of lightening up his attitude. He saw himself as a loser, like George Costanza from *Seinfeld*. I suggested he become more like Kramer- a goofy but happier individual. This was utilizing his good sense of humor to defuse the rage he often felt. He often came in feeling depressed and walked out laughing at himself and his overreaction to minor disagreements. Still, he needed to do more than just reframe things with humor. More depth was needed.

He was born into the Jewish religion but was not actively involved in Judaism. He did, however, relate to the concepts of Buddhism. He liked the idea that we are here for a reason and need to learn from every individual in our life. He started to view his wife as a teacher rather than just an annoying partner. He began to appreciate her good points and their relationship improved. The big change, though, was when he and his wife joined a Buddhist meditation group. Chanting a mantra (spiritual word or phrase) helps the mind let go of the external physical world for a brief period. Fifteen or twenty minutes at a time can help. The result is often a feeling of deep peace and calm. When practiced regularly it leads to an overall sense of well- being. Research has shown that there are even physical benefits, like lower blood pressure.

He described a shift in his energy and a change in his thinking after he meditated. The effect seemed to be cumulative. The fits of anger dissipated over a period of years. The depression lifted. He continued with the cognitive, humor-oriented therapy to solidify his gains. Most importantly, his outlook on life changed. He now views himself as leading a successful life. He appreciates his family, accepts them as they are and looks back on his teaching career as successful. He keeps in touch with his students on Facebook and feels he had helped a lot of young people in more ways than just by teaching them history. Many of them praised him as the best teacher they had ever had and he gracefully accepted their praise. He is a much happier person. His current challenge is to find ways to continue his meaningful life with his family and some part-time teaching. He continues with meditation and has a very forgiving attitude toward himself, his wife and his adult children.

Larry had been trapped in what I call the "vicious circle" of guilt, anger and fear. The underlying guilt and projection of blame on others to relieve the guilt of blaming himself, kept him firmly in the bipolar trap. The combination of cognitive therapy, humor therapy, and meditation enabled him to become closer to his Buddha nature and forgive himself as well as his wife. The anger was his most visible symptom but there was definitely a deep-seated sense of guilt (due to an unhappy childhood) underlying the depressive phase of his illness.

As mentioned earlier, guilt or shame is not usually seen directly. However, I find that by verbalizing a few common beliefs related to it, it is clear that it is pervasive. Some common guilty beliefs are, "I am not good enough," "I don't deserve to be happy," and "nothing ever works out for me." Such beliefs lead to the next troubling emotion, anxiety. The anxiety is about being punished for being guilty. I often use the analogy of a court of law in therapy. I say. "What happens in a court of law when you are convicted?" The patient always responds, "You get punished." And I point out that their anxiety is actually fear of being punished for their guilt or projected anger. Thus, I call guilt the root of all evil.

Buddhists encourage us to meditate and stop clinging to our desires. The four noble truths are; all life is suffering, suffering is caused by clinging and desire, clinging and desire can be released, the eightfold path can help release desire. In other words, suffering can be healed by following the Eightfold path. The eightfold path includes; right view, right intention, right speech, right action, right livelihood, right mindfulness and right concentration. The first two of these guidelines for successful living are designed to cultivate wisdom. . The third through fifth guidelines encourage ethical conduct. The last three promote inner change, through awareness and meditation.

Similarly, *A Course in Miracles* encourages us to pray for guidance from our real self. The real self is seen as merged with the reality of spirit. Forgiveness is seen as a psychological shift that leads us back to Oneness. Forgiveness is not what it is usually perceived. Usually we see it as a kind of holier than thou letting something go because they just don't "get it" (our point of view). Actually, says the Course, forgiveness is looking at the other person as a pure spirit, the same as we are. We all have the same source. If we behave badly, it is because we are seeing everything backwards. We are accepting the separated world as real, and denying a spiritual world or realm. As we truly let go of anger, fear and guilt we see the one spiritual realm as the source of our being. Another case will exemplify how cognitive therapy, Buddhist meditation and a lightening of negative beliefs leads to healing and radical personality change.

Harry's Story

Harry was a fifty-two-year old engineer suffering from severe depression. He was neglected by his angry, sadistic father and his mother who spent most of her time enabling his father's quiet rage. His father was so mean that he wouldn't even say hello if he passed him on the street and completely ignored him at home. He very much wanted to please his father but was unable to do so. As a young teenager, he began to be attracted to members of his own gender. He was seduced by an older boy and liked the sex. He realized he was gay but felt guilty about it. Thus he grew up with quite a bit of "gay shame."

At first, he acknowledged his father's cruelty but denied he had any shame about his sexual preference. He felt that his depression was caused by his inability to develop an intimate relationship. I pointed out to him that he had many intimate friends, just had trouble integrating sex into the relationships. Eventually he accepted that he did have a lot of guilt and shame, especially about sex. He also admitted that he hated his father and refused to forgive him. Thus, his depression was a mixture of guilt, shame and anger at his father. He needed approval though, so he rarely acted angry. He was the quintessential "good boy" who tried to please everyone. The guilt and anger were directed at himself-resulting in depression. Periodically he became very depressed and suicidal.

Early therapy was supportive with a cognitive orientation. He learned to reframe his experiences more positively. Instead of viewing himself as a loser at relationships, he saw himself as creating good relationships with most people and working on slowly integrating sex into his relationships with a person of his choice. He was OK, even if he channeled sex into masturbation. However, this was clearly not enough for him. However, he had not forgiven his father or himself. The turning point was his growing interest in Buddhism. He was very interested in travel and began to read about Southeast Asia. He visited there and became intrigued by the ideas of Buddhism. I pointed out a *New York Times* article by Buddhist scholar Robert Thurman entitled, "What Is the Point Of

Not Being Enlightened?" He loved the article and began reading books I recommended about Buddhism and therapy. He began to meditate and loved it. He practiced awareness meditation. He would just sit, breathe and watch his thoughts non-judgmentally. We talked in therapy about the Buddha nature. He felt he was getting there through the combination of therapy and meditation.

After a long struggle he began to forgive his father as well as himself. His relationships improved. He was even more helpful to his friends and family than he was before. This was due to his true compassion. He is much happier now than ever and is able to spot and let go of shame, guilt and anger as they arise. He has not had depression for a long time. He feels he is on the road to enlightenment. He is more peaceful, happy and stable than at any time before in his life. For him, forgiveness works!

If this type of therapy works, why do people resist it so much? Part of the problem lies in an inaccurate view of what forgiveness actually is. Whenever I give a talk about forgiveness, someone inevitably asks, "What about Hitler?" My answer is that they should forgive their family, friends, community, country, other countries and the last person they forgive should be Hitler!" People feel that forgiveness condones bad behavior. That is not the point at all. Forgiveness is showing compassion for the person whose own human issues led to such bad behavior. I often ask patients who are angry at their parents if they know how their parents were raised. They often know about how badly their grandparents treated their parents. "You see," I explain, "they were just like you." I often suggest that people imagine their parents as little children being abused and or neglected. This exercise often leads to more compassion for them.

In other words, we all need to see how we are all connected and have the same "issues." We can let go of our issues and begin a trend toward forgiveness. This letting go into forgiveness is fostered by a combination of cognitive therapy and spiritual techniques, such as meditation and prayer. The cognitive therapy logically leads us to compassion via insight into other people's point of view. The spiritual practice can reverse our view of reality. This reversal comes as a result of seeing Spirit or God as our source and primary to the vagaries of physical existence. No matter how we reach this conclusion, it is the result of experience induced by the spiritual/cognitive therapy. So we are still living as separate individuals in different bodies. However, we are focused on forgiveness and letting go of resentments. The combination of logic and spiritual experience and feelings has a remarkable, healing effect.

CHAPTER 8

The Culture of Narcissism: Are we Putting Descartes before the Horse?

"I think, therefore I am."

--Rene Descartes

The above quote from philosopher Rene Descartes seems rather obvious and innocuous at first glance. After all, we all think, and it does seem to prove that we are alive. As we examine the famous statement further though, it assumes a rather nihilistic view of human existence. It implies that at death, we stop thinking. Does that mean we are obliterated?

The quote above assumes that we are separate creatures each with a physical brain, and that thinking is a purely physiological brain process. As long as that brain thinks, it proves we are alive. Is there anything more to a human being? Existence seems to be defined as conscious thought alone. This is all we are. To quote Dr. Karen Horney, centuries later, we are "alone and isolated in a hostile world." We are subjects-physically split off from everything else. In fact, there is a major branch of modern psychoanalytic psychology called "object" relations. This makes human beings into separate "objects" that relate to each other. Other cultures, often considered more primitive than us, saw things differently. Native Americans, for example, saw themselves as extensions of one Great Spirit. The European white man, however, in his arrogance, considered the "rational, enlightened" view of Descartes and many others as superior to the views of indigenous cultures. Western Culture, and its people, have suffered ever since.

To A God-Centered Life

Most people don't think philosophy has much to do with their lives. But it does. In fact, our unseen philosophical premises are the bedrock of how we view the world. If we see ourselves as separate creatures, threatened by others, competing with others for survival, there will be inevitable conflict and suffering. Even if we are not immediately threatened, we will think we are. We band together with our families, tribes and countries and fear other families, tribes and countries. If we have anything, we fear that others will forcibly take it away. If we have nothing, we may be jealous and want to grab things from others who have a lot. Individually, we will compete for Earthly comforts, pleasures, prestige and success. Each person wants to be like the man in Frank Sinatra's song "New York, New York:" "A -number one-king of the hill, top of the heap." A few people reach positions of power and luxury, even though they usually don't enjoy it. Most others assume they would be happier if they were at the top. Few people simply just accept life and enjoy who they are.

I am making a radical proposal here. I am proposing that we all shift from a materialistic, narcissistic, egotistical philosophy of life to a God-centered life, based on spiritual values. This does not mean necessarily obeying a lot of rules. It simply means valuing peace, love, compassion, forgiveness, joy and gratitude over money, material gain and prestige. For a humorous song about switching to spiritual values, go to my web site, www.drmenahem.com.

Doing things God's way embraces a spiritual way of living. Humor and music can heal many human maladies, including loneliness. Both humor and music are, in my mind very spiritual. It helps us "enlighten up."

CHAPTER 9

Loneliness: Is it the human condition? Can it be healed?

How many people can claim that they have never been lonely? Rare indeed is the person who has not felt lonely or blue. My mind just jumped to the first few days of my two-year U.S. Army stint. There I was in South Carolina, ripped away from my friends, family and familiar surroundings. I was drafted to fight in a war I believed was wrong. I was being trained to kill people I didn't even know. I felt angry, scared and cut off from the other people around me. I even felt spiritually bereft. If there was a God, I wondered, how could he let this whole scenario occur? At first, there seemed to be little hope of any immediate relief. Life seemed to be a matter of survival from the angry sergeants, yelling at me, threatening to "kick my kneecap off" if I did not obey orders.

Gradually, though, things improved. I soon realized that the other soldiers were just like me. I began to make connections. I began to realize the importance of friends. I had always made friends easily. This was a big plus in my readjustment. I realized that loneliness can sometimes be cured by relationships. The sense that we were in in the same leaky boat bonded us together. I didn't realize it then, but it was a spiritual thing, a sense of connectedness that healed most of us from our loneliness.

The Origins of Loneliness

Psychology can give us some insight into the origins of loneliness. The great psychoanalyst Dr. Karen Horney wrote that poor parenting, especially from a self-absorbed, narcissistic mother could create "basic anxiety," a sense of being "alone and isolated in a hostile world." The neurotic "cure" for this unhappy condition could be compulsive pleasing, compulsive achievement or compulsive distancing from other people. If people pleasers feel cut off or lonely, they try to find people to connect with and try to get them to like them. Achievers try to know everything and be better than everyone else. "Distancers" don't usually feel lonely (though they may feel so deep inside). They find solace and safety in being cut off and alone.

None of these solutions really works. The "pleasers" and "achievers" are particularly prone to loneliness. They try to become their version of the ideal person but this does not help them to be happy. They lose their real self in the chase for so called "glory." Connectedness to others must come from the "real self. "According to Horney, compulsive, neurotic solutions need to be gradually dropped. This puts you on touch with your real self-spirit. Horney believed that psychoanalysis could strip away the neurosis, enabling the "neurotic" to love other people as well as themselves.

Although psychotherapy has come a long way since Horney wrote her epic book, *Neurosis and Human Growth* (1951), I believe that, in essence, she was right. Compulsive, neurotic defenses keep us cut off from our true self, which is spiritual. It also cuts us off from honest, healthy, relationships with others. It is a cultural myth that only a romantic relationship can take us out of loneliness and into happiness. People vary in how much they need others to feel connected and whole. A mature person, however, can feel connected and happy in a spiritual way. Spirituality is nurtured by finding some way to connect to the divine. I almost always inject an element of spirituality to lonely patients. Meditation, contemplation and prayer often help. I treat a lot of older patients, who complain that all their friends are dying off. I direct them both to God or spirit and then back to others. Loneliness can be helped by connecting to the God self, the real inner self and then too reconnecting to others in a healthy way. Clinginess is rarely appreciated by people of any age. But, healthy sharing of mutual interests does help cure loneliness. Horney might say that when people share their real, spiritual selves, a healing occurs.

Spiritual relationships are not found only in church or synagogue. Like many other issues I've discussed, I find that humor is one of the best ways to connect with oneself and others and cure loneliness. Patients often leave my office laughing. That in itself is not the cure. However, one thing I try to model is that we all take ourselves far too seriously. To me, enlightenment means lightening up. Loneliness dissolves when we are one with our real selves. We can then feel happy, connected and healthy-instead of lonely, isolated and misunderstood. Music can also help cure loneliness. Both music and lyrics can bring us up out of self-pity and away from feeling cut off, isolated and lonely. So don't emulate "Mr. Lonely" in Bobby Vinton's classic hit song. Instead, find a spiritual practice, drop neurotic defenses and get in touch with your real spiritual self. Learn to laugh, love unselfishly and be happy with whoever you are and whoever you are with!

Speaking of music, lyrics and happiness, here is a piece I wrote recently that expands upon music's ability to heal loneliness and all kinds of psychic pain.

CHAPTER 10

Meaning, Spirituality and Rock and Roll

Everything we need to know about finding meaning in life can be found in lyrics by the Beatles. It isn't that the boys from Liverpool knew something no one else knew, but they were able to popularize and package ancient truths in a way that was palatable for millions who may have never come across some of these truths if not for their lyrics. "Beatlemania" had put many strains on John, Paul, George and Ringo. Sometime in 1966, the Beatles came under the influence of the founder of TM, Maharishi Mahesh Yogi. In addition to learning how to meditate, the Maharishi's work influenced their work, specifically in the song "Within You, Without You" written by George Harrison for the Sergeant Pepper album. The song, with a background of sitar music by Ravi Shankar, takes us through the basic ideas of Hindu Vedanta Philosophy of life. We are here to experience the bliss of oneness with God. This is love in its purest, universal form:

"We were talking, about the space between us all,"

People put up" walls...

Of illusion, never glimpse the truth, then it's far too late..."

Life is seen here as an illusion (maya) by the Hindus. By getting quiet and meditating, we may avoid taking the external illusory world too seriously. The song advises us to be in the world but not of it. Once we experience the joy of this underlying love, we can show others the way. According to George Harrison, love is the answer to inner peace!

A Word about Change

The Beatles advise us to realize that change is difficult and cannot be forced on us by anyone else. We have to realize that we are part of a grand process and allow positive change to happen. As soon as we tap into this universal love, change becomes not only easier, but more natural. The change is from selfish material values to a search for meaning in helping and healing others. We have to learn to look to spirit for answers. As we learn to share our love with others we will find peace in making love. They were not referring to physical love making. Rather they were talking about connecting in universal love! Only then can we see true meaning. Thus, the last two lines of Harrison's "Within you and without you: are,

"And the time will come when you see we're all one
And life goes on within you and without you."

This song may also be seen as a brilliant psychological technique. It begins by getting the listener's attention with an outline of the commonness of feelings of alienation. Listeners are urged to go inside themselves to find the reason for their alienation. The song asks ask if you, the listener, suffers from this alienation problem? If you do, then the answer is to develop a selfless, loving attitude and share it. Your selfish striving for attention will drop away and your life will be meaningful.

All You Need Is Love

Though "Within You without You" is the clearest indication of spiritual philosophy in the Beatles music, it is certainly not the only one. Later in 1967, they were asked to write a song for their BBC special which would reach all over the world. Lennon and McCartney sat down and wrote a simple little song that said it all, "All You Need Is Love."

"There is nothing you can do that can't be done,
There is nothing you can sing that can't be sung...All you need is Love."

This song went beyond individual unhappiness and focused on the violence and hatred in the world at large. In 1967, we were tormented by wars all over the globe. All the strife was caused by needless hatred of one group by another. People were killing people for economic gain, or the ownership of their particular brand of truth. Often it was all pursued in the name of God. All this, say the Beatles, was and is for naught. The answer is so simple, all you need is love. Just do it!

The Beatles are not the only musical group that gave us insight into the healing of the human condition. Bob Dylan, The Eagles, Don Henley, and Friend and Lover also helped us understand life.

Dealing with Death

Existentialist philosophers like Nietszche and Kierkegaard stressed the importance of dealing heroically with your own death. Their idea was that we have to take responsibility for our lives and live the best life possible even though we will be extinguished at death. Later, other existentialists such as Paul Tillich, a theologian and Psychiatrist, Dr. Victor Frankl felt the same way, despite a different view of what happens after death. These more theistic philosophers felt that death is not the end.

Dr. Frankl, who spent several years in a Nazi concentration camp, felt that there was always a reason to improve one's attitude and continue living. Tillich, in his book *The Courage To Be*, felt that death was the root of all anxiety and had to be faced courageously. Both of these philosophers agreed though that despite the fear of death, death was not the end. This sentiment has been echoed in rock music as well. Bob Dylan wrote a song called, "Death is not The End." The song concludes:

"Not the end, not the end

...Just remember that death is not the end"

Hotel California

Don Henley and The Eagles, one of the most popular Rock groups of the 1970s and 1980s, wrote a song that can easily be seen as a metaphor for the life/death experience. The fictional "Hotel California" was a place where you could live it up. It was on a dark, dusty highway, part of a long trip. When you get there, you can do anything you want. You can also try to get away, but there is no escape:

"You can check out any time you want,

But you can never leave."

Think back to the clinical example of Chuck in Chapter One. He wanted to "check out" and escape his issues. I convinced him that he could check out, but never leave.

For those who believe in reincarnation, that we have a succession of lives, this echoes the philosophy of many people. According to Buddhist and Hindu philosophy, we lead a series of lives, each of which is an attempt at spiritual growth. We have many experiences according to the "law of karma," or the law of cause and effect. We reap what we sow and until we have compassion for all sentient beings, we have to return to Earth for another life. Thus, we have the prophetic nature of the "Hotel California." We are condemned to stay at the Hotel (life) until we learn to love properly. Then and only then can we escape. There is no way to avoid spiritual growth, so we might as well accept our stay in the mythical hotel and learn to be more loving and compassionate.

Forgiveness

As I've discussed earlier, forgiveness is a major theme in spiritual growth. Without forgiveness we tend to hold on to grudges, resentment, anger and hate. Relationships are ruined this way. People are usually more interested in being "right" or getting revenge than in reaching inner peace and forgiveness. On a larger scale, lack of forgiveness leads to international difficulties, including war and terrorist attacks. This theme has been picked up by many rock and roll songs.

Don Henley, former lead singer of the Eagles, considers forgiveness the essential element in healing a relationship. In his song, "The Heart of the Matter," he begins by mourning the end of a love relationship. He thought he would find someone better. Only in retrospect, can he see that he was mistaken.

"I've been trying to get down to the heart of the matter but my will gets weak...
...But I think it's about, forgiveness, forgiveness...

Here, Henley realizes that the only way for both of them to move on in life is with forgiveness. He sees how many people are filled with rage and feels only tenderness and forgiveness can help. He also sees that pride and competition cannot help us be happy! Only, forgiveness can bring us peace, happiness and contentment. In the final stanza, he suggests that "if you keep carrying that anger, it will eat you up inside." Only with forgiveness can they both move on and have happy, healthy lives.

Essential Truths about Relationships

The song, "Reach Out in the Darkness" also carries some essential truths about relationships. In this case, they are singing about hate relationships. It is a little known truth how close hate is to romantic love. In romantic love relationships, we tend only to see the good aspects of the other. We idealize them and they do the same to us. We are temporarily unaware of our faults, as long as the loved person is with us. Psychologist Dr. Ken Wapnick says that we have temporarily put a lid on our self-hate. However, inevitably, the loved person pays less attention to us and the "lid" loosens. We protest because we don't want to see our flaws or self-hate. Then, we blame the other person and our love changes to hate if they don't respond to our demands for exclusive attention and to be the way "we used to be." As the song, (written by Jim Post and popularized by Friend and Lover)" says:

"I met a man that I did not care for

And then one day this man gave me a call,"

After discussing their issues, they become friends.

When we do not like somebody, it is usually because they remind us of qualities in ourselves that we do not like. This is called projection. Psychiatrist Carl Jung taught us that we project onto others the qualities we don't like in ourselves. This is the "shadow." According to Jung, it is important to work out relationships with those we dislike so we can see our shadow, accept those disowned qualities, and become whole. In the process, we just may turn some of those enemies into friends. By forgiving the other, we can communicate and turn the hate into friendship. We have to reach out in the darkness of the shadow and learn to love ourselves and others.

What the World Needs Now

Anyone living anywhere in the world knows that there are massive problems confronting humanity. Many people are starving, homeless or victims of war and civil unrest. Some people are losing their jobs, homes and visible means of support. Others are losing their retirement savings and can no longer afford to retire. Still others are drastically altering their life styles to barely make ends meet. Entire countries are going bankrupt. Credit and interest are almost non-existent. In other spheres of life, the reports are equally bleak. Global warming is melting polar ice caps and causing the seas to rise. Cities may be under water in just a few years. The entire world trembles before a few terrorists who blow people up in the name of God. Many live in fear that a terrorist might get a nuclear device and kill millions at once. Economically, politicians are printing more money-temporarily hoping that the "economy" will turn around. Environmentally, energy sources are disappearing. Alternative energy sources are slow to develop. In order to fight senseless killing, terrorists are captured and tortured in an effort to control hatred. Are these ultimate answers? Or are they stop-gap measures? What would you do if you had magical powers to fix everything? What does the world need now?

I believe Dionne Warwick gave us the answer in her 1960s song: "What the world needs now, is love sweet love."

In other words, we need a massive shift in consciousness. We need to let go of fear, anger and underlying guilt (unconscious self-hate). As soon as we let go of these things, the love, underlying physical reality will take over. This is not a romantic love, as depicted in pop culture. Love is the universal Godly force that connects all physical beings. This is the ground of being or Buddha nature that is our ultimate source. Normally, as physical beings, we are not really in touch with our deeper, spiritual nature. We are primarily concerned with physical well-being (health), pursuit of pleasure, and avoidance of pain. Physical needs drive us. We are afraid we will not get what we need-food and shelter or what we want-pleasure, prestige, luxury. We may also be angry that what we need and want eludes us. Finally, we may feel unworthy, due to guilt, of getting what we need and want.

Obviously, there needs to be a shift in the consciousness of masses of people. We all need to find ways to let go of guilt, anger and fear. *A Course in Miracles* teaches us to let our inner teacher or guide us in this endeavor. As we practice each of the lessons, we gradually learn to let go of guilt, anger and fear. As we let go, a new form of consciousness evolves. If we treat each other and the Earth kindly, we feel better. As we realize that we can make more money, and spend the money we have confidently, we will not fear the economic future. Rather we will tap into the natural abundance that can be drawn to each of us through the law of attraction. But the law of attraction is not simply visualizing a Lexus. It is about realizing that spirit is the primary reality. God is. Love is. I am that I am. The material world then becomes a training ground for the fundamental laws of the universe, spiritual laws. We develop a spiritual consciousness and spiritual values. Success is then defined not by our bank accounts, but by the kind, loving way we live our lives. Try to reframe your life. You will like it!

As this "spiritual-cognitive shift" occurs for more and more people, the physical world will make a comeback. But that is not the main point. *A Course in Miracles* teaches us that the physical world is simply a reflection of our inner state of mind. As our material needs are met, we can shift our energy into spiritual values, the true source of happiness. We are here to practice forgiveness! We are all here to shift from materialism to spirituality. Let's go!

CHAPTER 11

Taking the "Self" out of Self-pity

"Poor me...poor me...pour me a drink." This is one of the many catchy mottoes from Alcoholics Anonymous. But you don't need to be an alcoholic to wallow in self-pity. Lately, it has occurred to me that much of what we call moodiness, the blues, or despair is really self-pity. We are looking at our current life situation, perhaps comparing ourselves to others and coming up short. We feel helpless to do anything about it and slump into the morass of feeling sorry for ourselves. Perhaps a fresh look at this pervasive malady will shed new light on a very old problem. I would like to look at this unfortunate condition through three lenses; the skeptical, monotheistic and spiritual (monistic) viewpoints. The three views of humankind have one idea in common. We must take the "self" out of self-pity in order to heal. How we get the "self" out depends upon how we view life.

The Skeptical View

I will define a skeptic as someone who doubts that there is a God. Skeptics fall into two groups. Atheists profess to **know** that there is no God, agnostics simply doubt it. Both groups, however, see human beings as primarily separate, biological creatures, competing with each other for scarce resources. Survival goes to the fittest and brightest. Natural selection weeds out the weak and unfit. Life is therefore seen as a struggle of physical bodies to survive and prosper due to a combination of hard work, talent and confidence. From this point of view, we are either "winners" or "losers." Even the "winners," however, often think they are not doing well enough. Thus, there are many more losers than winners, in terms of how people feel. There is a strong tendency to become self- absorbed and self-pitying in such a paradigm. After all, the only thing that matters is surviving and "winning" at the game of life. This means more than just accumulating wealth. It means that things should always, or almost always, go your way. If you think you are a good person, and most people think they are, then you should be guaranteed health, wealth and little or no misfortune. Anyone who sees life this way is bound to be at least moderately narcissistic and could easily fall prey to feelings of self-pity when things are not going right.

At this point I can relate the self-pity I felt immediately after my previously mentioned medical crisis. I remember my dismay after having the sudden heart attack in 2002. I thought, "How could this happen to me? "I am thin, have normal cholesterol, exercise, eat a vegetarian diet, have a good attitude and am a good person. How could I get a heart attack while that other guy who is fat, lazy, atheist and depressed doesn't?" Wow, if that wasn't self-pity, what was? I realized I was making what I call "the deal with the empty chair." I felt that if I did everything right, I should never get sick. "Why me?" might be the motto of the self-pitying person.

The key to the self-pity is that there is nobody in the other chair making such a deal. The deal was all in my head, based on the "good boy who does all the right things" solution to inevitable problems in life, especially from the materialist, skeptical point of view. Not only that, although I believe I am spiritual, my body became the focus when I got sick. I reverted to the skeptical, materialist point of view. My spirituality became "spiritual materialism." I wanted God to heal my physical body, NOW! From a material point of view, I began to think that that health is a very complex thing. The controllable factors like diet and exercise do not guarantee anything. There are also genetic, environmental, and unconscious psychological factors which may be beyond our control. We may even be in denial about certain related factors as I will explain in my own case.

I was in denial about the importance of dental health on my heart. I did not floss and refused to use the prescribed dental rinse because it contained an antibiotic. Bad move. I also have a genetic inflammatory disease called Familial Mediterranean Fever (FMF). There is a preventative medication, colchicine. I refused to take it. In my prideful way, I wanted to be medication free. Thus, I had an FMF attack five days before the heart attack. I saw no connection. I now believe that inflammation from the gums and FMF were the physical triggers to my problem. I could have done something, but didn't know about the connections. I am not blaming myself. It was a combination of lack of knowledge and denial. However, even if I had all the knowledge and physically did "everything right," it still could have happened. Health is not totally controllable. From a skeptic's point of view, one should take as much control as possible and let go of the results. Acceptance of uncontrollable factors, like genetics and environment, is part of taking responsibility for one's life. It is the mentally healthy way of dealing with problems in living. For skeptics, taking responsibility, not blame, for one's health and accepting what happens to you takes the narcissistic self out of self-pity. From this point of view, self-pity can be healed.

The weakness of this system, however, is that it places inordinate pressure on the conscious ego. How much knowledge does one have to have to survive? How much self-care is enough? When should one take a pill? Go to a doctor? Run to the emergency room? Exactly how and when does a person surrender to fate and the uncontrollable factors in life and health? These are difficult problems indeed and cannot be completely solved without going outside the ego-body system. Thus, I have been impelled to go beyond the body and ego into the realm of God and faith.

The Monotheistic View

Yes, God is the answer to healing self-pity. But who or what is God and what does God want of me? Traditional monotheistic religions like Judaism and Christianity view God as a super being that controls everything. In the Old Testament, the loving God keeps trying to teach his disobedient creations, from Adam onward, to love and revere him. Then, everything will be wonderful. As we know, human beings keep disobeying orders and keep getting punished by God who is slow to anger, but does get angry at his creations. Of course, we humans never get the point and keep going our own "selfish" ways. Thus, we get repeatedly punished by the angry God who loves us and just wants us to get the spiritual point; love him and each other and then he will be quick to forgive.

The New Testament tries to correct the vision of an angry God by emphasizing the perfect love, Jesus, God's son, had for humanity. Of course, people still did not listen and he died for our sins. That is the traditional interpretation. However, monistic interpretations, like the contemporary *Course in Miracles*, differ on the meaning, as we shall see later.

It is very helpful in healing self-pity or healing anything for that matter, to believe that a loving God is on your side waiting to help. Prayer becomes the vehicle we use for the healing. We ask God to do the healing. We may or may not have to do anything ourselves. But we go outside the ego system of total self-reliance and ask a higher power to help us. Thus, we are not alone and isolated in a hostile world of uncontrollable factors. Help is available. Healing is ours for the asking. Further, death is not an obliteration of who we are. We are essentially an immortal soul, just temporarily housed in a body. When the body dies, we are simply released into an invisible, spiritual realm, sometimes called Heaven. The idea is to pray for guidance, listen for answers, perhaps take some action, or maybe just have faith and trust that whatever happens will be for the highest good of our soul.

For anyone with faith, this is a big improvement over the skeptical materialist, courageously facing his inability to control his eventual demise and obliteration from a meaningless, random world. There is a reason why religions continue to flourish in an increasingly complex, scientific, and materialistic world. A belief in God gives people hope that their life has meaning. It takes the pressure off the constant need for vigilance and control. The higher power, God, understands and knows things that we humans do not know. Thus, the development of faith is a key element in healing self- pity. The ego self can do some things to survive and prosper in the physical wprld, but the real power is in God.

Most skeptics say that they would like to believe in God but can't understand why a loving God would create and maintain a world such as ours, full of suffering. The answer, given to us in the book of Job, is that we do not understand everything and we must learn something through our suffering, faith and trust in God. Out of the worst suffering comes spiritual growth. Perhaps even physical death leads to a better state of being. This is the lesson of traditional religious belief. The problem with monotheism is that it seems to imply a separation between humankind and God. Thus, monistic spirituality-a belief that we are all One with God- is more helpful. With monistic spirituality, physical death is not a big issue. It is not physical death that releases us into the experience of God. It is understanding and experience that elevate us into oneness, peace and love.

The Spiritual View

The Oneness of God is always there. We are one in God. In truth, we never left this unending source of love, peace and bliss. The very nature of the one source of all being is immutable and immortal. Our experience on Earth, however, is nothing like this heavenly state. Instead we are dogged by a gnawing sense of fear, anger, guilt and danger. When things don't go our way, we get angry and petulant. These emotions are very disturbing, mentally and physically, so we develop defenses to keep them out of our awareness. We automatically repress most of the disturbing emotions. What we cannot repress we consciously suppress. What we cannot suppress or repress we outright deny and project onto other people. It is as if we are saying, "My unhappiness isn't my fault…it is your fault." We may blame others, the "bureaucracy," the government or even God, anyone but ourselves. Such denial and projection, of course, leads to conflict. Individually we have disagreements, screaming matches, even physical fights. En masse, we have wars. The very existence of the planet depends on not blaming others, withdrawing our projections, stopping our denial and repression and recognizing what is really going on at the psycho-spiritual level. In reality, we are feeling separate from our Source, God and thus feel separate from each other.

The answer to all our problems, including the indulgence of self-pity, is reconnecting with the Source, experiencing the peace and love of the Source. This reconnection involves a true "ego-self-ectomy." The recognition that the ego-self is a made up concoction of cognitive and emotional experiences of a lifetime is a shock. The "you" that you think you are, is actually a series of learned beliefs based upon your experiences as a separate individual.

We are taught from the beginning that we are nothing but a separate person having sensations and experiences in a body. Our natural tendency is to cling to that which is familiar. It is familiar to feel alone and isolated in a hostile, competitive world. Most of our everyday experiences reinforce this view. It is very hard to see that our beliefs create our experiences. We feel that the experiences just randomly happen to us. Then we create the belief system that we are just conscious egos in bodies, trying to survive. We have everything backwards.

A brief look at developmental psychology confirms the idea that our belief systems are learned. With great difficulty and trauma, we learn that we are separate from others at the physical level. We learn strategies to "survive." The first half of most lives is concerned with developing beliefs that seem to insure survival and perhaps success. At mid-life, most people take it as fact that we are separate in body and mind. We do not realize, however, that our very separation and individuality is the cause of our suffering. Instead, we feel that we are somehow inadequate or unworthy of happiness. We think it is a personal failing, not a species wide mistake that makes us suffer. Or that we are helpless victims in an uncaring, brutal world. Either way, at mid-life, we face a choice, we can continue to stubbornly reiterate and re-experience the materialization of our beliefs and continue to suffer. Or, we can choose to dis-identify with our beliefs and see what else there is to us. In the absence of any scientific "proof" that there is any more to us than the obvious ego-brain-body-idea, most people choose the former. However, there are some who simply intuit that there is something more to us than just a brain-body that dies and becomes nothing. For this smaller group there are many places to turn.

There are many traditions that tell us that life is a spiritual adventure. Among them are the ancient Advaita (no two) Vedanta, Ancient Kabbalistic Judaism, the Existential Metapsychiatry of Dr. Thomas Hora, The Infinite way of Joel Goldsmith and the contemporary opus, *A Course in Miracles*. For the purposes of this chapter, I will merge these philosophies into a spirituality of Oneness.

According to the writings of Rabbi Isaac Luria (16th Century) the physical word was started by an explosion (called-Tzim-Tsum in Kabbalistic Judaism) of God. The energy source, God, withdrew from itself, creating an explosion. Matter was created there, as an extension of God. This means that all is still one. However, the vessels designed to hold the contents of the explosion couldn't take the heat and seemed to shatter into shards of matter. We humans, indeed, the entire physical world, is composed of these seeming shards of Godly matter. This is the spiritual big –bang theory. The explosion part insinuates that the seeming separation is not real. The seemingly separate shards are still part of God. They simply need to be raised back into the oneness through human thoughts and deeds. In Judaism, fervently following 613 laws (mitzvot) of good conduct, spiritual values and loving kindness (kavannah) raises the sparks and re-institutes the Oneness.

This coincides well with *A Course in Miracles* mythology. Using more Christian terminology, a perfect, loving, peaceful God is rolling along when a "tiny mad idea" occurs. Some part of the Oneness falls under the illusion that it could split off and set up its own kingdom, the material world, separate from the Source (God) and independent of God. In reality, this is impossible, but it seems to be real. Within the material world are people, who have no idea what happened and follow along with the worldly program of individual existence in material form. The problem is that once the illusion seems real, it engenders sin and guilt. The guilt is about a metaphysical "running away from home" and thinking it is independent of the Source (father) when the truth of it is that it could never really be separate from the source and is just fooling itself. The guilt is about disobedience.

Then there is the fear of Godly retribution (amply demonstrated in the Jewish Old Testament). Guilt, however, is too painful to feel, so anger is created by denying any responsibility for this mess of a world and blaming it on someone else (other people, or God). This in turn creates more fear that God will retaliate angrily. The rest is human history. People feel alone, isolated and are suffering, and denying any responsibility for it. In particular, they deny that their suffering has any connection to God or spirituality. They would rather see the material as real and God as non-existent non-caring or punitive. Thus, we have the human situation. As I see it, the spirituality of Oneness is the only way out of this self-created trap.

Both *A Course in Miracles* and Dr. Thomas Hora agree that experiencing the love and peace of God can be accomplished. The path is to use your life as a giant lesson plan. Each time you suffer, think of what spiritual lesson or value is being learned. Then, instead of retreating into self- pity, depression or anxiety, make the shift in thinking that is required. It is a spiritual-cognitive shift. According to the Course, we must learn to see all of humankind as One and the same-Spirit. This enables us to practice forgiveness and the development of "holy relationships." This is the only reason we are on Earth having physical experiences.

Dr. Hora says there are only two intelligent questions; "What is the meaning of what seems to be?" and "What is what really is?" I believe that answering these questions at each and every upsetting experience will lead us into the experience and understanding of spiritual values and spiritual living. It will enable us to really be forgiving of others and eventually ourselves. If we keep choosing peace, instead of the seeming "rightness" of our material obsession, we can attain a life free of self-pity and full of peace, love, and gratitude.

CHAPTER 12

What is Happiness?

"Happiness is a warm gun."
--John Lennon

When I was in the U.S. Army (1969-70), John Lennon was enormously popular. The former Beatle had just chosen Yoko Ono over our beloved Beatles. His shift from the Beatles to Yoko was to prove fertile ground for some of his best work. When I was stationed in Germany, a fellow GI had just returned from Vietnam. He liked the Beatles too, especially the line quoted above, about happiness being a warm gun. He assured the peace-nicks in our medical/dental unit that indeed, it made him happy to have a warm gun in his hands. We all hooted him down, called him a war mongering idiot and told him that Lennon was referring either to sex or drugs. These were two things, we assured him, that Lennon was much more familiar with than an actual gun.

A few months after my discharge, I was happy to catch Dick Cavett interviewing Lennon. Cavett asked him what that line meant. He replied that it meant exactly what it said. A warm gun gave him a feeling of power. The warm gun wasn't a metaphor at all. I was shocked, dismayed, and wanted to look up my GI friend and apologize. Now, I think Lennon was just being flippant and kidding with Cavett. I still think he wrote that line as a metaphor of sorts. John was talking about sex within a loving relationship. He also sang, "When I put my finger on your trigger...."

Was this a metaphor? Perhaps he felt most loving while making love to his beloved Yoko. He later wrote, "Oh Yoko...I love to turn you on..." Lennon had been abandoned by his mother when he was a baby. Later his aunt Mimi abandoned him. He felt very unloved and sought happiness through fame and fortune. He got both of these things (as well as a lot of sex and drugs) as a Beatle...but he was not happy...until he met Yoko. No matter that the press called her the "dragon lady. " He felt loved by her and expressed it. Much of his solo work in the 1970s reflects this change in attitude. He extended his love from Yoko to humanity with his classic song "Imagine." He sang:

"Imagine all the people, living life in peace...You may say I'm a dreamer...but I'm not the only one, I hope someday, you'll join us... and the world will live as One."

Now he went beyond just loving his wife. He was visualizing a world that was warm, peaceful, loving...joined as One, in the spirit of God (though he never uses such a religious word). In his later years, living in New York with Yoko and son Sean, he was much happier than he was as a famous Beatle. Happiness is a warm feeling called love. Our society worships romantic love. But I think Lennon realized that romance was just the beginning. We must connect in peace and live as one.

> "Happiness is a warm puppy."
> --Charlie Brown

Charles Shultz is the author of the above Peanuts quote. He created an enormously popular fantasy world, the comic strip, "Peanuts." These "Peanuts" were children, looking for love and often not finding it. Charlie was always lusting after the little red haired girl (his yearning for a special, romantic relationship) and getting no satisfaction. He was also always scolded by mean old Lucy (perhaps a metaphor for Charlie's vicious superego?). But there was one thing that Charlie loved: a warm puppy. What was so great about a puppy? Well the answer is simple. It is warm, cuddly, non-judgmental and not demanding of anything in particular. Puppies want what we people want, someone to love them. If we love them, they love us. Puppies exude unconditional love. How simple. Is it too much of a cliché to say that the kind of love we can feel with a warm puppy is what humanity needs? I think not. The reason Peanuts was so popular is that it taps into the obvious in all of us. We just need to love ourselves and each other like puppies love us, in a non-judgmental way. We are already good enough. With our own self approval, we can then spread love to others. Carl Rogers, with his "client centered" therapy, told us the qualities in an ideal psychotherapist; warmth, genuineness, spontaneity and exuding unconditional positive regard. Yes, just accepting and appreciating another has a healing function.

Two widely different individuals, John Lennon and Charles Shultz taught us the same basic lesson. If you want to be happy, love and accept yourself and others. Learn to sincerely and spontaneously make the inevitable lemons of life into lemonade. Don't judge or criticize yourself or others. Then, happiness, without being pursued, will land softly on your shoulder, like a butterfly. No "mind games" are necessary for happiness sings Lennon. There is no need to project any particular images on anyone. As The Dalai Lama said, "be the love you want to see" and you will be happy.

CHAPTER 13

What is Spiritual Reality? Get Real!

"Wake up and smell the coffee!" This common dictum is meant to encourage people to get out of their state of avoidance and denial and do what they have to do to manage their life. Perhaps it is an encouragement to pay overdue bills, or get out of a bad relationship or go to a medical doctor. At any rate, the statement is meant to arouse the recipient to take some physical action. Now, sometimes actions *are* necessary. However, the reference to waking up to the reality of the physical world can lead to a denial of the spiritual world, the real reality!

Free Rent

In 1973, my wife and I moved to San Diego for graduate school. There, we met Gene and Evalie, a young married couple. Gene was studying to be a "missionary pilot." He wanted to fly all over the world and spread the good news about Jesus-from a fundamentalist point of view. Shortly after we all met, Evalie became pregnant. She was having a difficult pregnancy and had to stop working. Since she was the wage earner, we asked how they were going to survive financially. They both smiled and said, "God will provide!" My wife and I were shocked. Was God going to pay the rent ($135, the market rate for San Diego in 1973). We said nothing.

Several months later, she gave birth. One day we saw some people helping them move out of their apartment. We asked what was going on. They replied that one of his classmates was letting them live in a cabin on his farm for free! All they had to do was help with some farm chores. God indeed had provided what they needed, in answer to their prayers. It was my first experience with that kind of faith, and answered prayers. I quickly forgot about this incident as I pursued my studies as a psychologist, grounded in psychodynamic and cognitive "reality." I would take on life being a responsible person, taking care of myself. God receded into the background. I thought I knew what reality was. I could smell the coffee. I thought the free rent thing was just luck.

I never took God or prayer seriously until 1989. As I wrote about in chapter three, "We Have Everything Backwards," I was dealing with an angry, depressed, suicidal patient who blamed everything that had gone wrong in her life on me! As you know, after I started praying, I began to believe in the importance of prayer in healing.

Spiritual reality had interacted with physical reality to produce a result that was asked for. It wasn't a case of a superman in the sky, interceding. Instead, it was the result of focused intention, interacting with the creative energy of Spirit, creating a different reality. God, which is "All that is," had followed the instructions of my thoughts, feelings, beliefs and prayers, creating an event that would insure that the dysfunctional "therapeutic" relationship would end. It may have been the only way for both of us to move on.

In Hindu theology, the law of karma implies a balancing in a relationship, due to cause and effect. Karmically, it was the best we could do in this life to balance our relationship. Resolving karma does not always mean that all parties move on easily and peacefully.

In other words, I had everything backwards. I had thought that physical reality was all that is. Then I thought a super-being controlled physical reality. Then, I realized that through an interaction of Spirit, mind, emotions and physicality, our lives unfold, as they are supposed to, in order to learn our spiritual lessons. God is all that is-the energetic source of physical life. The intervening beliefs, thoughts, feelings are the filters that create the particular forms of life that the world calls reality! Spiritual reality is actually all that is. It encompasses sense perception, many layers of unseen "beingness" and transcends all of the "layers" of being. Physical reality is just one offshoot-a manifestation of feelings and thought patterns.

What we call life is the dreamlike trance that seems so real, we assume it IS true reality. Spiritual reality-the Oneness of all life-is the energetic "beingness" that transcends and *IS* everything. To quote Wayne Dyer, "We are spiritual beings, leading a human life, not human beings with a spiritual life." God, the Buddha nature is All That Is. We are living, not to gather the most stuff we can before we die and are obliterated. Rather we are here to embody the highest spiritual values; forgiveness, peace, universal love, happiness, gratitude. As Dr. Thomas Hora, creator of "existential metapsychiatry" said, "The problems are psychological, but the answers are spiritual." That is because life is spiritual, whether we accept that or not. Spiritual reality is the *source* of so called physical reality.

So I urge all readers to wake up and smell the spiritual coffee. If you don't like your life, change your belief in what reality is. Make the *spiritual-cognitive shift* from material values to spiritual values. Live a life devoted to forgiveness, love and peace. Then will you know and realize spiritual reality.

CHAPTER 14

Do We Create Our Own Reality?

The question of whether or not we create our own reality has been central to my thinking since 1977, when I was an inquiring young psychologist. I was already working with people as a therapist. My theoretical orientation, however, changed often. My friends in graduate school would kid me by asking, "Hey Sam, what is the therapy of the week?" Then, a few years later, a trip to the mall changed my life. I was waiting for my wife to finish shopping and went into a bookstore. Instead of heading to the psychology section, I decided to go to the "occult" area, where a purple book with a weird picture on the cover caught my eye. It was entitled *Seth Speaks*. I picked it up with the thought, "Let's see what kind of nonsense this is." I started reading and thought ... "Oh this is good." Then, I flipped a few pages, read a bit more and thought, "This is good too." Soon, I was engrossed in this book, whereupon, my wife walked in and said, "I'm tired, let's go home!"

So I bought the book. As soon as I got home, I started reading. I had the next day off and finished the book in one day. I was stunned. It seems that "Seth" was a "non-corporeal energy gestalt, not presently focused in physical reality." "He" spoke through a medium called Jane Roberts. Neither Jane nor "Seth" had studied psychology, but it was the best psychology book I had ever read. It basically said, "You create your own reality, through your beliefs, conscious and unconscious, period, there is no other rule!"(Roberts, 1974) "Wow" I thought, "now

I understand what I am doing with my patients: helping them change their beliefs."

Changing Reality

Now, skeptics might say this is just cognitive therapy. But what Seth suggests is more than that. It is not only reframing the events that have already occurred, it is changing the actual events in our perceived reality, even to the point of healing physical disease. According to Seth, "Your body is a living sculpture," and each of us is our own sculptor! So I started playing with this idea. For example, I began to change my belief about the difficulty of parking in New York City. I changed, "It is hard to park in New York City" to "A good parking spot is waiting for me." As you might guess, I get a lot of good spots, and now, everyone wants to drive into New York with me. Later, when I went for job interviews, I decided I was the best candidate. I would affirm, "Who could they get for this job that is better than me?" I would usually be offered the job.

I began to use this belief changing process with patients also, and it worked! I realized that the difference between positive thinking (which I learned from my grandfather, mother and father), and belief change. Beliefs are deeper than thoughts. Our thoughts flow out of our beliefs. Therefore, no amount of positive thinking will override a negative belief. First, the belief has to be changed. Then, you can affirm your new belief. Seth, channeled through Jane Roberts, explains this in his best book, *The Nature of Personal Reality.* He tells us not to just believe what he is saying, but to try his belief change techniques. "If you don't like your life, try changing your beliefs about life." Further, he tells us to use our lives as *"a playful experiment."* He encourages us to "imaginatively pluck out the troubling belief and replace it with what we really want." The process for belief change is, recognize the negative belief, face it, pull it out by the roots, and finally, replace the negative belief with a positive one. This is summarized by the phrase, recognize, face, replace."

A whole new world opened up as I used these techniques. Here's another personal example. Despite the negativity of medical doctors about my wife's ability to have a child, I rejected this negative belief and used positive beliefs, affirmations and imagery, accompanied by positive emotion, that we would have a child. That was 31 years ago. We have a wonderful 31-year-old daughter!

Obviously, I discovered that we have more control over our reality that I ever thought. Nevertheless, I also realized that I was not practicing magic. I did not always get what I thought I wanted. This was due to one of four things: my own hidden or unconscious negativity, negative emotions (anger, fear, guilt), negativity around me, or that my wish was not for my highest good. In other words, I needed humility to understand life better. Too much control is grandiose and narcissistic. None of us is mature enough to always know what is for their highest good, or the highest good of the world at large. The world is not just there to please any one individual. We need a great deal of strength and maturity to deal with group disasters like 9/11 and hurricane Sandy.

The "serenity prayer," from Alcoholics Anonymous, tells us to change what we can change, accept what we can't change, and the wisdom to know the difference. I needed to learn that life is not just about creating a good life for me. It is a group learning process. Improving my personal life was just a stepping stone to the realization that life is created from the spiritual level. It is fine to want and create a better physical life, material wealth, and psychological happiness. But I was soon to learn that there is much more than that.

Seth shows us how to improve our daily experience by changing our beliefs. To a large extent it works. Then we realize that true happiness is beyond just improving our belief system. It lies in waking up from our narrow focus on "stuff." and opening up to spiritual enlightenment. In other words we need to make a huge cognitive shift, from positive beliefs about the physical reality we experience to the knowledge that we are really One with Spirit, or as Seth calls it, *"All That Is."* This may sound like an arduous journey. But my experience is that enlightenment means lightening up. We can pursue Oneness with our source with

Seth's playful attitude. We can enjoy our process of giving up harsh judgment and criticism and replacing it with laughing at ourselves and our stubbornness.

As I continued to read and incorporate the Seth material into my life, I realized that it is very similar to the previously mentioned, *Course in Miracles*. The Course has us look for the Holy instant for Salvation, Christian terminology. Seth teaches us to playfully change and improve our beliefs, with the underlying knowledge that we are part of "All That Is," having incredible experiences on many levels of reality at once. In other words, we are wonderfully creative. We are learning spiritual reality from all of our connected selves (Seth's version of reincarnation). Life, according to Seth, should be joyful, creative and loving! The Course says that we should turn ourselves over to the Holy Spirit, forgive everyone, and realize the joy of being one with Spirit. Compared to the ego driven life, defending itself and its fragile body, Seth and the Course are marvelous alternatives. So do we create our own reality? Yes, if we are coming from the level of Spirit and the real self. No, if we are coming strictly from the ego-body level. So, if you don't like the reality you are co-creating (with Spirit), change your beliefs!

CHAPTER 15

Freud Meets Jesus

Sigmund Freud was a great pioneer in the field of psychology. He is responsible for the introduction of the importance of the unconscious in human behavior. He also formulated the ideas of id, ego and superego, eros and thanatos, resistance, transference, ego defense mechanisms, separation-individuation and the importance of trauma in psychological problems. Freud was a physician, trained in neurology and psychiatry.

Working with another physician, Dr. Josef Breuer, he treated many women with so called "hysterical symptoms." These women were suffering from paralysis or blindness with no known organic cause. He developed the idea that by going into their past and having them remember sexual traumas from early childhood, they could be cured of their symptoms. In his early years, he used hypnosis. However, he was a poor hypnotist and soon developed the "free association" technique. The patient was instructed to say anything that came into her mind. Eventually, she would remember the trauma and go through a cathartic abreaction (re-experiencing the emotion). This emotional catharsis was the cure. It was a very controversial treatment (it was late nineteenth century Vienna) but seemed to work in many cases. That was the practical side of his work. However, there was also a theoretical side, the creation of an entire metaphysical system called psychoanalysis. Freud's psychoanalytic theory formed the backdrop for most subsequent psychotherapy.

The Three Energies

According to Freud, all human beings are energized by a powerful, unconscious energy called the "id." The "id" is really "das es" in his native German, meaning more literally the "it." The id, he said, is a result of metabolic processes. In other words, it is a physical, instinctual energy, shared by all human beings, who were first and foremost, physical beings. The id is a powerful force, characterized by sexuality (eros) and aggression (thanatos). Hence, young human beings want what they want, and they want it now! What they want is sexual pleasure and power, as well as complete control of their physical environment. Since all of these goals are unrealistic, and narcissistic, the young child needs to be controlled. It is the parents' job to provide appropriate limits and teach the young child to control him or herself.

The sexual and aggressive impulses are pushed down or "repressed" into the unconscious mind by the demanding superego. The superego is a set of rules for conduct taught by the parents. The child's selfish urges don't really vanish. They are just hidden and may emerge as symptoms or behavioral problems. Repression is an automatic process. Anything that is not automatically repressed is to be controlled by other defense mechanisms, especially denial and projection. In other words, when we are caught being too aggressive or sexual, we deny it or blame someone else. However, the superego is a little harsh sometimes. Id impulses are very powerful, so a new part of the mind develops. Freud called this the "ego," (Greek for "I"). The ego is the conscious part of the mind that seems to be who we are. It is composed of both id and superego elements. It is the conscious mediator between these two powerful forces. It only wants to be aware of acceptable impulses and needs to defend itself from both id impulses or drives and superego demands for proper behavior. Thus, it needs defenses to keep an acceptable front in place while secretly gratifying wishes for sex and power.

This conscious part of the self, the ego, is always afraid. On the one hand it is afraid of the powerful sexual id. On the other hand it is afraid of the mean, punishing superego. Thus, the job of the ego is to mediate between the demanding, sexual-aggressive id and the harsh, parental superego. Psychoanalytic therapy was originally an "id" therapy. As the theory developed, however, it became an "ego" therapy. Freud stated that the goal of psychoanalysis was to develop a strong ego, to ease the id-superego battle and live successfully and happily in the real, physical world. He wrote, "where id was, ego shall be." Psychoanalytic therapy was designed to develop a strong, flexible, ego. The job of the ego, the part of the self we are aware of, is to be good citizens, channeling the powerful instincts into acceptable means. A mentally healthy human being, according to Freud, would have many healthy coping mechanisms or ego defense mechanisms, like rationalization and sublimation to protect it from id impulses and superego demands. The psyche contains id, ego and superego elements. The more elements we are conscious of, as egos, the healthier we are. According to Freud, we are primarily our conscious selves, egos. We, said Freud, are physical beings, living according to the dictates of the ego, which wants to be safe. Safety, to the ego, requires many techniques of keeping the other parts of the mind at bay and dealing with the demands of physical life, which is the only real thing.

Where's God?

There was no room for God or a higher power in this system. God, to Freud, was an illusion, a sort of super parent image that didn't really exist. According to Freud, any mystical feelings of oneness are simply regressions to a prenatal state of physical oneness with the birth mother. Spirituality was reduced to an unhealthy regression to the womb, in order to control anxiety.

A Course in Miracles, already introduced in earlier chapters, presents a very different view of reality and life than Dr. Freud. In many ways it is a complete reversal of Freud's beliefs. It is written by the metaphysical Jesus or Holy Spirit and brought into the material world. It completely reverses Freud's view of reality. According to The Course, we are one with the godly energy. At some point, a "tiny mad idea of separation arose." This separation led to the delusion that we are separate from God and merely physical creatures. All guilt, fear and anger are caused by this central delusion of humankind. This idea is completely the opposite of the Freudian notion that we are physical creatures, driven by instinctual physical energy and suffering from the anxiety of trying to adapt that overpowering energy to living in the real world. According to the Course, the ego is the enemy of peace. As long as we listen to the mad voice of the ego, we will never be happy. I believe the Course's ego is what Freud called the id, ego and superego. Regardless, according to Freud, the ego is who we really are. There can be no ego without a body. According to the Course, the body and the entire physical world is simply a dream, an illusion. How different can you get? Thus, Freudian metaphysics and the Course are diametrically opposed to each other.

Although they are so radically different, there is one thing they have in common: the psychodynamics of the Course bear a startling similarity to Freud. Let us delve a little deeper. Leaving aside the issue of the reality of the ego, all human beings need to be mindful of this ego and how it operates in the phenomenal world of separation. The Course is very clear that as long as we think we are separate egos, we are prone to deny and project the primary emotions of guilt, fear and anger. Guilt, says the Course, arises with the separation. It is very disturbing to be fundamentally guilty. According to the Course, we are guilty of wanting to create our own world, independent of God's world. This guilt is so powerful that we need to deny it completely. But we are secretly afraid that God will find out about our separate inclinations and punish us, maybe even kill us! So to avoid this painful guilt and fear, we deny that there is a God. We deny that we are afraid. We deny that we are guilty. If anyone challenges our denial, we get angry, maybe even righteously indignant. We then live in a vicious circle of guilt, fear and anger, which we must deny or find someone else to blame. Maybe we even blame God -if we believe in God-or just the government, big business, the world or cruel fate if things don't go our way.

Strangely, Freud had similar conclusions, except that he said we are afraid not of God's wrath but of our sexual and aggressive instincts, which are unacceptable to society. We then try to control the instincts, and become afraid that others may find out we are really very selfish and driven by sex. So we deny our unacceptable impulses or blame them on someone else. To Freud, the unacceptable impulses have nothing to do with God or spirituality, it is about unacceptable sexual and aggressive impulses. To the Course, the unacceptable impulse is to be separate from God in the first place, which then leads to all suffering. The best a Freudian can hope for is a fragile peace between warring parts of the self, which must defend itself from others knowing its true intentions. For the advocates of the Course, there is a much more hopeful answer. It is called the Atonement.

Here's how the Atonement works: We are instructed to turn inward in prayer and receive guidance from the inner teacher or Holy Spirit. We will then be guided to total forgiveness. We will realize, with time, that we are really one with God. As we pray for a change in perception, we will notice that we are all one spirit, sharing in our source. The "holy instant" is when we realize this "At-one-ment" with God. We can then give up all fear because there is no real death. There is only eternal spiritual life. What we thought was "life," physical life, was just an illusion. We are eternal, loving and peaceful. The nightmare is over. To Freud, we have to live within the nightmare, which is the only reality. Then we die forever and are extinct. To the Course, we wake up from the dream of separate bodies, guided by egos and full of guilt, fear and anger. The Course's reality is a wonderful true metaphysical reality. Which one do you prefer? I think I'll study the Course!

CHAPTER 16

What I think Jesus Really Meant

I was recently asked to give a Sunday sermon at a local, Unity church. Although I accepted the invitation, I didn't know what to speak about. As I prayed for an answer, my inner voice directed me to take some quotes from Jesus and explain what I think he really meant. This was quite a task for a Jewish kid from Brooklyn. Here are the quotes, and what I said about them that morning:

"The kingdom of heaven is at hand."

Most people think this quote from Jesus Christ, aka Rabbi Yeshua of Nazareth, means that when you die, you go to heaven -if... you were good. I take it to mean that you can be happy right now, while you are still in your body, living on this Earth. You need to take responsibility for your decisions, accept the consequences and make the best decisions possible for you. In other words, we need to own our own power and surrender when things are out of our control. When you go through events that cause pain and suffering, you go within and pray for a way to re-frame the event. How can you learn from it? What part does it play in the great cosmic lesson plan of life?

"Love thy neighbor as thyself."

Most people think that we should just be good to others, but what about the people who hurt you? What about mean people? What about hateful people? What about bullies? What about terrorists? I believe Jesus meant that at the deepest level, we are all the same. Our source is God, the father. We all appear to be separate creatures, with separate bodies. But we are much more than that! We are souls who are at the deepest level all connected, and in the same human predicament. How can we survive and prosper in a seemingly unfair world full of difficult people, horrible diseases, poverty and natural disasters? I believe Jesus meant that if we experience the sameness of all people due to our common source, we can develop deep empathy, caring and love. Through loving others-we can find our true humanity. Even bad guys can eventually be forgiven.

"Forgive them! They know not what they do."

This is spoken by Jesus about the Romans, who were about to nail him up on the cross and murder him. They considered him a dangerous agitator who was rousing up the masses against Roman authority. Most people think that only Jesus could reach such a level of forgiveness. Actually, we are all capable of great forgiveness and compassion, especially if the perpetrator of bad deeds doesn't know any better. The Romans had little understanding about spiritual matters. They were all about worldly power. Jesus, a Jew, knew that the main point of life was for loving God and your fellow man. He knew that death was no big deal. Thus, he willingly forgave the Romans. In fact, they were giving him a chance to demonstrate immortality.

He said to himself. "I'll just die on the cross, come back in three days, teaching my followers that when you die, you are not dead." Thus, people will no longer fear death. He may not have even felt a lot of pain on the cross. Some people can hypnotize themselves so they produce a kind of anesthesia, and I assume Jesus could do it too. Thus, he did not suffer and die for our sins. On the contrary: he was trying to teach us to be better people, without fear of death, in a dramatic fashion!

"These things I do…you can do greater."

He performed many miracles, including healing the sick, raising the dead, and feeding the poor with loaves and fishes. Was he really saying that ordinary people can do this? Yes. What he meant was that every person is really a son or daughter of God. We all have the potential to do great things, even miracles if we realize our Godly source at the deepest level. We are then given powers, commensurate with our level of maturity, love and compassion. Immature people, who would just brag, boast, and selfishly claim ego-based fame are not ready for such miraculous powers. They would use their power selfishly and maybe even dangerously. But once we mature, and come in intimate contact with God, we can do the kind of miracles he did.

"Tis not I that doeth the works, tis the father within."

When we develop our powers to succeed in life as healers, helpers, and workers, we must treat our abilities and successes as gift from God. We must realize that God has gifted us and refuse to gloat or think we are better than others. People who do that are narcissists who immaturely feel they are superior. Instead we are to remember our source, God. We then share our gifts and skills and help others. This is true humility. This is not to be confused with low self- esteem. With humility we know we are good, know that our good comes from God and share the wealth. We know that we are all good, just in different ways.

"You shall know the truth…and the truth shall set you free."

The truth is…we are all One with God. At the soul level we are the same. We are here to learn this truth, feel its ramifications, and learn the great cosmic lesson plan. The plan is to love God, love each other, and help each other out of deep compassion. We must realize that we were all damaged in childhood and that if we or others behave badly, it is because of those early wounds. Then we can forgive, let go of toxic emotions like hate, shame, and fear and let God fill us with joy and abundance. We can then accept our Earthly healing and move on to the spiritual level in peace. That is, we can be happy in Heaven. We don't need any more Earthly incarnations...unless we come back to strictly help others learn the truth.

CHAPTER 17

The Secret behind The Secret

Several years ago, Rhonda Byrne wrote a book called *"The Secret."* It turns out that *"The Secret"* is not really a secret. It was basically a repackaging of an idea that has been written about under many names for at least two hundred years. It is usually called the "Law of Attraction." I was introduced to it by my grandfather, who bought a series of positive thinking books by Robert Collier, a popular self- help author in the 1920s He gave them to my mother, who used Collier's ideas to "send the waves" when anyone in the family was ill. In ancient times, this was called prayer. Often it did help, but not always.

This was the beginning of my wondering why some people healed, while others did not. Later, my father gave me *The Power of Positive Thinking* by Norman Vincent Peale, and *Psycho-Cybernetics* by Maxwell Maltz. Both of these books talked about how to regain health and wealth through positive thinking and changing negative to positive beliefs. Thus, I was programmed to be interested in the power of positive beliefs and thoughts by both of my parents. This is the secret! My own psychological training and inquiry into healing led me to become a spiritually-oriented psychologist. I traced healing and the power of thought back to the late 18th century. The healers I studied included Franz Mesmer (the first hypnotist), Pierre Janet (a better theorist than Freud in my humble opinion), P.P. Quimby (a miraculous American healer), Mary Baker Eddy (Founder of Christian Science) and Ernest Holmes (Founder of

Science of Mind). This "new thought" movement spread all over the world. In 1920s France, for example, Emile Coue had half the country saying, "Every day, in every way, I am getting better and better." It worked for many people but not for all. Why?

My studies continued with the previously noted, *Seth Material*. Seth explains why some people heal and some don't. I also found out why some people are financially successful and some are not. Finally, I found out why some people are happy and some are not. It was right there, channeled by an "entity" called Seth, As previously discussed, the main idea is:

> *"You create your own reality, through your beliefs, conscious and unconscious, period, there is no other rule."*

This is the real secret. It was the simple answer to my search. Cognitive psychology was revealed to me by a spirit. I finally knew what I was doing with my patients. I wasn't just listening to them complain or report their personal news. I was helping them see the powerful effect of their beliefs on their lives. I was helping them change their beliefs from negative to positive, thus creating positive thoughts. The negative, disharmonious thoughts had emerged out of their buried negative beliefs. Most of this process was unconscious, but could be made conscious.

Seth was combining Freudian, psychodynamic therapy (make the unconscious, conscious) and cognitive therapy. Utilizing these theories, I was helping people to take responsibility for creating their thoughts, emotions, health, and abundance — in short-their lives. I have been doing this for forty years. The secret is not really a secret at all.

Laws of Attraction

While I was glad to see *The Secret* was clearly stating the law of attraction, I was a little disappointed that people were reading it and putting too much emphasis on external abundance. "Think positive, get stuff," is not the spiritual message we really need. I was also disappointed that people were naïve in using the secret to approach the healing process. People heard, "Just change your thoughts and you will be rich and your cancer will go away." Well, as I learned in childhood, you sometimes need more than just someone telling you to think differently. I would like to provide a few more steps and techniques that I think are important, which seemed to be glossed over by the people watching the video of *The Secret.*

First, if we are dissatisfied with our lives, we must examine our conscious thoughts and feelings. Be aware that our beliefs lead us to thoughts and these thoughts are often connected to feelings of fear, anger, and guilt. We are like buildings made of bricks (beliefs), cemented in by mortar (feelings). We can loosen the mortar (feelings) and rebuild our houses with better bricks (beliefs). We must take responsibility for the fact that we have each built our life out of our experiences. Instead of blaming others, the world, God or circumstances for our woes, we must *take responsibility for this house we built (with our belief system).*

Second, we need to be less selfish and more giving. *We must take responsibility for our lives by developing forgiveness for others and for ourselves.* We need to do this out of compassion for the suffering we all endure due to our negative beliefs, especially the belief that we are all separate from each other and from God. In truth, we are all connected on a deep level. Understanding this spiritual truth leads to a great belief change. We are very attached to our separate identities. We want what we want. We also don't want negative outcomes. This is natural. But we need deeper insight than we normally have. The insight is to recognize the deep spiritual connection between all people. We must turn to our inner spiritual teacher (higher self, holy spirit, soul) instead of our ego, for guidance in daily conduct.

Buddhists have the same basic idea. One of the Four Noble Truths is that all suffering comes from desire (clinging to separate identity). As mentioned in an earlier chapter, the Buddhist cure consists of the eightfold path, which includes right mindfulness, right thinking, right speech, right livelihood, right view, right effort, right concentration, and right intention. In other words, as we meditate, with positive intention, we see that we are much more than our thoughts and feelings which emerge out of attachment to separate self. We are urged to practice non-attachment. That is our responsibility. Once we accept this responsibility for our way of thinking (clinging, desire, negative beliefs), our lives begin to change. We see the world differently. But how is this done? It is done by releasing; meditation is a releasing practice.

The third step is learning how to release judgments and negative emotions (anger, fear, and guilt) which hold negative beliefs in place such as "I don't deserve to be happy." Guilt holds this negative belief in place. Meditation is one way of releasing such negativity. Another way to release negative beliefs, thoughts and feelings is the "The Sedona method," which I've described in Chapter 5. As a reminder, it suggests asking ourselves three questions. "Could I release it? Would I release it? If so, when?" If it feels like we can release it, we do. If not, we ask again later, until we feel it releasing. We can then replace negativity with a positive belief via imagination, or even better, by just letting the natural power of our inner spiritual teacher develop the positive belief for us. The ultimate positive belief, which is really beyond all beliefs, is that we are all Spiritual beings, unique manifestations of the same one source, often called God.

This is the ultimate "secret," we are one with God, joined in Spirit. As we realize this we will naturally love our neighbors as ourselves because our neighbors are our selves.

CHAPTER 18

You Are a Money Magnet

Cozy Michaels is a friend of mine since childhood. He is a terrific drummer and has his own band in south Florida. While I was visiting my mom in Florida, I invited him over to visit. He was in severe financial distress. Beneath this distress, of course, was a set of very limiting beliefs that blocked his way to getting enough work. After some small talk, he launched into his tale of financial woes. I listened for a while and then I said, "Hey Mike, are you a chick magnet?" He answered, "Oh yeah Sam, you know that. Women love me!" (They do love him). So I added, "Now I want you to pretend that you are a money magnet!" He laughed and said that affirmation. Then I added, "Now say it while using your middle finger to tap the top of your head. (The idea of tapping certain places in the body to help change beliefs comes from "energy psychology(EFT)", a new branch of psychology. The tapping helps the positive energy flow.

Now Cozy was really laughing, as he and I and my brother Lew, tapped away. Shortly after he left, he called and said, "Sam, you are a genius, that technique worked. I came home and had two messages, asking for gigs! Now I can pay my rent!" Now, I am not a genius, but I do know how to use "the secret" or law of attraction in a way to create both financial abundance and spiritual values. Here are the directions I mailed him to keep the momentum going:

Financial Abundance Directions: Must be followed exactly
For Cozy Michaels

1. Enclosed find two twenty dollar bills. Take the one that says. "You are a money magnet." Sit and meditate while looking at it for exactly five minutes first thing in the morning, and exactly five minutes before bed at night. At various times during the day, you must repeat the mantra, "I am a money magnet," while tapping the top of your head. Do this for exactly 21 days. On the 22nd day-you must spend $20 on something pleasurable.
2. Take the other $20 and find a homeless person. Give him the bill and say "May God Bless You. Get something to eat!"
3. Be aware of your feelings and thoughts as you give the homeless person the money. You must open up to the idea that you deserve an abundant, happy life, while also finding ways to serve your fellow human beings with the money you magnetize to you!

Love,
Dr. Sam

Cozy practiced and was very excited. He was especially glad about the reaction of the homeless man, who kept repeating "God Bless You." There were inevitable backslides, as he needed to really change his beliefs and self-image as a "poor" person. But he is learning and still uses the technique.

I often use the technique with patients and with my classes at Columbia University. The experience of one patient, who I will call Jacqueline, a dog walker, stands out. One day Jackie was in an elevator, about to take a puppy for a walk. As she descended, she began to tap her head and repeat, out loud, "I am a money magnet." When she got outside, she looked down, and there was money on the ground, $401 with a rubber band around it. She looked all over for the owner, so she could give it back, but nobody was around. So she kept the cash! Jacqueline is also using the technique to drum up more business and develop a career as a Reiki healer. Now, as I tell this story, I caution the people that usually you have to **work** for the increased money. But, if you practice, and believe that you deserve a happy, abundant, spiritual life, in which you share the wealth, then it will come to you. This is the real secret behind The Secret!

CHAPTER 19

Can We Really Change? Or Are We Just Stuck The Way We Are?

When I was a young man (a long time ago) I was shy, introverted and had an inferiority complex. I did satisfactory work in school. However, every teacher thought that I could do better. I thought I was trying hard, but my efforts were futile. I thought that I would never do well enough to satisfy my teachers or my parents. At home, the son of my mother's best friend beat me up daily. He was a strong bully and always won. My mother told me not to fight him, but this was impossible because he attacked me. So I concluded that I was weak, dumb and generally not good enough. Over the years, I changed. Thank God!

I gradually concluded that I was smart enough to go to college and do reasonably well. I didn't think I was smart enough for a doctorate, but one school admitted me and I was aided by a very wise teacher, Dr. Alvin Marks. The first day of class in my dissertation seminar he said, "How many people here have at least a one hundred IQ?" I raised my hand, along with everyone else. He continued, "...that is all it takes, plus a lot of perseverance." So I persevered and ended up in a field I was very well suited for, psychology! I got my doctorate and became a psychotherapist. This was quite a change from the shy, inferior child I had been. What were the factors that fostered the positive changes to that point?

First, I was aided by my parents who told me I could achieve in school. Even though I didn't believe I was smart enough, they did. Second, I was helped by my many close friends. I had always been able to make friends and keep them. For the most part, they were very supportive and helpful when I expressed self-doubt. I will never forget my friend Barry forcing me to apply to graduate programs when I was stalling. He was there when I found the one Ph.D. program in San Diego that accepted me. Third, I had some very good psychotherapy, early on. When I was floundering after college, my mother sent me to her therapist. The therapist concluded after two sessions that I needed a male therapist. My mother's therapist knew that my mother dominated the family and felt I needed a strong male figure to model myself after. That was when I went to Dr. Leon Charney. Dr. Charney, a wise, compassionate and funny man indeed became my role model. I will never forget his plethora of supportive stories that helped me face my challenges and move ahead. For example, when I mentioned I was good with people, he suggested I do what he did, psychotherapy. I responded, "You mean I could help people and get paid fifteen bucks for it?" It had not occurred to me that I could be a therapist.

Fourth, I learned how to make the best out of bad situations. In 1968, despite my beliefs opposing the Viet Nam war, I was drafted. While in the Army, I decided to maintain my anti-war beliefs, without doing anything illegal. For example, along with many of my fellow soldiers, I signed a peace petition that appeared in the New York Times. I also placed an anti-war quote of the day on the bulletin board and played Phil Ochs anti-war songs for the troops waiting for medical exams. When ordered to take the music off, I did, but at least I got to play it for a while. I did very well as an anti-war soldier and was proud of it. I also discovered that I could make people laugh! People laughed at my antics no matter what. In short, getting away from home I was able to really become my true self. To my surprise, I liked this self. Dr. Karen Horney would say it was my "real self."

Fifth, I became open to divine guidance early in my career. I became interested in meditation, the power of prayer, the psychic level of being, spirituality, and synchronicity. Every step of the way I was presented with fortuitous opportunities to advance my career as a spiritual psychotherapist. I accepted the challenge to be one of the people leading the field of psychology in a spiritual direction. I joined together with like-minded therapists and started the Association for Spirituality and Psychotherapy (ASP). I was now a leader in the field of spiritual psychotherapy. Thus, my own journey has shown me how much a person can change in the course of a lifetime.

People Can Change

My experiences with patients have been equally reinforcing of the idea that people can change. In fact, I have seen miraculous changes in many people who have come to me seeking help. One man, the aforementioned Harry, who was frequently suicidal, developed an interested in Buddhism. As I constantly reminded him to turn to his Buddha nature-Oneness-in times of trouble, his spirits improved. He is a much happier man now than ever before!

CHAPTER 20

Can We Heal Ourselves?
Or do we need help form another person or spiritual presence?

As I mentioned in the chapter on self-pity, I had a serious heart attack in 2002. As I woke up in a hospital bed, a doctor was asking me, "Where are you?" I wasn't sure where I was. My arteries were so blocked that I needed two stents to keep them open. This emergency surgery was done by an expert cardiologist. As I opened my eyes and saw my wife and daughter I could only think, "Thank God I am alive." "What happened?" I gasped. "You had a heart attack," said the doctor. I couldn't believe it. I exercised, meditated and ate a vegetarian diet. How could this happen? And how do I recover? I was too weak to think much at that time. I did have that self- pity, but I also had gratitude that I survived.

As I gained strength, I began to pray for myself: "Thank you God for saving me and bringing a complete recovery of health." The phone started ringing. I answered, saying "Center for miraculous healing, can I help you?" I felt increasing gratitude for all the wonderful friends and family who visited and prayed for me. My synagogue prayed, the entire local Episcopal Church prayed. My friends at ASP prayed. Even my agnostic best friend prayed. Gradually I felt stronger. I give great credit to God for the healing. I thank all my friends for their loving prayers. I thank my expert cardiologist. I thank him every year now. He recently told me I was doing great and my EKG was "awesome." As I think of all the good things that have happened since the heart attack, I am increasingly grateful for my life! Did I do the healing myself? Or did I need all these other people and the spiritual presence of God?

Clearly, I needed the doctor who re-started my heart and did the surgery. Thank you Dr. Angeli. Clearly I also needed the love and prayers of my family and friends. Thank you all! Clearly I still need my own optimism and positive thinking. Thank you Norman Vincent Peale! Clearly I needed God's positive answer to my prayers.

But wait, according to *A Course in Miracles* and Buddhist philosophy, this life is all really a dream. Philosophers from Plato to Miguel de Unamuno espoused the same philosophy. There were even two 1950s "doo wop" rock songs with that philosophy, "Life is but a Dream" and "Sha- boom." Myself, my doctor, my friends are all really part of the great Oneness of God. I "dreamed" a heart attack and recovery. But the entire experience has allowed me to increase well- being through spiritual realization. I can let go of anger, fear and guilt more easily than before. I can forgive others and myself more quickly than before. I am a better, therapist, teacher, husband, friend than before. So maybe my near death experience was just all part of my "great cosmic lesson plan," the movement toward enlightenment. So on the earthly level of reality, we do need others and a spiritual presence to heal. But the greatest healing is the enlightening knowledge that we are all really one with God. Now if I can only get all the way to enlightenment. Maybe I should enlighten up. I am writing more jokes, and trying to see the positive in everything. To quote Louie Armstrong, "I think to myself, what a wonderful world." That is sage wisdom, indeed. Thank you Satchemo!

Did you hear the one about an Asian man who walked into a bar? He had a cat under one arm and a guitar under the other. The bartender asked him who he was. Oh, said the man, we are the band." Really, said the bartender, what do you call yourself? Oh, answered the man, we are the cat-man-duo.

CHAPTER 21

Reincarnation and Karma in Psychotherapy

The twin concepts of reincarnation and karma, if properly understood, can be enormously helpful to people working out their issues in psychotherapy. It does not matter whether it is a relationship issue or a symptom like anxiety, depression or phobia. The problem is usually a long-standing one, which has recently intensified in some way. At any rate, the person is temporarily overwhelmed and seeks assistance from a therapist. Unconsciously, the new patient wants symptom removal or relief without any effort or inner change.

A good therapist will start by helping the person feel understood and see the problem clearly. The therapist will proceed to help the person see how she created the issue by habitual negative behaviors, thoughts, emotions and attitudes. That is the easy part of therapy. The harder part for the patient is to look inside, overcome resistance to change, and make the underlying changes that will truly heal the issue. This is not a mechanical process. It requires realizing that negative beliefs and negative emotions must be released. The patient must stop denying and projecting her problems on others or the world at large. Each patient must become highly motivated to make behavioral and cognitive changes, despite inertia and resistance to change! The process of psychotherapeutic change can be facilitated by exploring reincarnation and karma.

A proper understanding of the reincarnation and karmic process leaves the psychotherapy patient with two options. She can face her problems now, or wait. She now knows that the problems will not just go away with the passage of time or eventual death.

The Framework of Reincarnation

Reincarnation is the doctrine that each human being has many lives. In other words, we are much more than just our bodies; we are ever-evolving souls. Each soul is an energy gestalt that reincarnates many times in order to change negative personality patterns into positive ones. The positive patterns we seek are greater love, compassion, kindness and selflessness. We do not move toward selfless goals for selfish reasons. Rather, we naturally move in that direction as we begin to grasp the true spiritual nature of human consciousness. A shift from selfish values to more spiritual values leads to a happier, more peaceful life — even if we have less money or stuff.

Traditionally, only religion was available to help people cultivate and value selfless love, however, there are a few psychotherapists who have integrated spiritual values into psychotherapy. A few of these pioneers were Dr. Carl Jung, Dr. Viktor Frankl and Dr. Thomas Hora. More recently, Dr. Brian Weiss has been particularly influential in utilizing spirituality gained through past life regression. If we look at life as a spiritual search, the role of the therapist is to be a spiritual catalyst. The purpose of therapy is no longer mere symptom removal. Viewed from a spiritual perspective, our problems become opportunities for character development and spiritual growth. We may have many lives to develop, but develop we must. According to the spiritual philosophy of reincarnation and karma, we retain free will. We can move ahead now or waste many lifetimes being overwhelmed by problems, some of which are carried over from previous incarnations. Although we don't usually remember past lives, we may have vague memories that manifest themselves as negative personality patterns and symptoms. In fact, we probably choose our parents and general life circumstances in order to work on and transform the old negative patterns into newer, more positive ones. This philosophy is expanded upon in the Jewish Kabbalah and The Seth Material.

The framework of reincarnation extends the therapeutic growth pattern over many lives. The therapist is still helping the person deal with very real problems in this life. The wider context however, makes seemingly mystifying problems like phobias much clearer and solvable. That's because you understand that your symptoms might be the result of something that has happened in a past life. The motivating inclination is that no matter what your life is like, you must face your problems sooner or later. If you keep avoiding them, they will follow you into another life! Understanding the wider framework gives the person hope that, through understanding, she will be making progress toward a wider goal. The potential for growth now becomes unlimited. Life will not end after a finite number of years, snuffing out the hard therapeutic work.

Most western people are not familiar with these concepts so they must be introduced to them in a rational, balanced, palatable manner. The best way to start is to explore a person's current beliefs on life, death, survival and meaning. For the purely materialistic, scientifically minded person, the mounting evidence for reincarnation can be explored. A book like *Reincarnation* by Cranston and Williams would be a great start. The authors of this volume explore the various kinds of evidence for past lives. Included are past life memories in children, hypnotic age regressions, near death experiences and cases of unexplained genius. There is even a section on reincarnation in various religions. This search is not limited to Buddhism and Hinduism. There is also an exploration of Jewish Kabbalists and Gnostic Christians, both of whom believe in reincarnation. As reincarnation is introduced, explained and the evidence is weighed and examined, it is more likely for the patient to become open to more hopeful conclusions about life. However, reincarnation cannot be fully understood without its companion concept, Karma.

Three Kinds of Karma

Karma is the universal law of balance and justice. You might recognize some popular expressions of the law of karma: "As ye sow, so shall ye reap." "Do unto others as you would have them do unto you." "If you spit in the air, it comes back to you." "He who lives by the sword, dies by the sword." In other words, you can't really get away with anything. If you limit this concept to your current life, it doesn't always seem to work. Bad things often happen to good people, and sometimes bad guys seem to get away with their misdeeds. Actually, nobody really ever gets away with anything. By broadening the concept of karma from the viewpoint of reincarnation, we can see that a seemingly "bad" event may be the result of something done in a previous life. This is not just a meaningless payback. Rather it is the way people learn that the spiritual, compassionate way of life is the goal. Troubling events are part of the curriculum to correct bad behavior, thoughts and feelings. Since there is a result for every deed, feeling or thought, why not be kind and compassionate, think good thoughts and cultivate loving feelings toward others as well as yourself. We are all part of the same, One, loving consciousness! Karmic payback is not really a punishment. It is a correction of error. *Karma provides balance and justice that eventually lead the soul to compassion and forgiveness for all misdeeds to others and oneself!*

The more stubborn a person is throughout the souls incarnations, the harder the lessons get. The more one sees the lessons in the "bad" things that happen and changes his ways, the easier the lessons become. This brings up a key point, which is especially important to those with a passing knowledge with the concept of karma. Most karma is changeable. Even in cases of unchangeable karma, there is freedom to choose one's attitude toward their fate! Basically, there are three kinds of karma: karma of action, karma of belief and karma of destiny.

Action Karma

Action karma refers to one's habitual ways of behaving. It may refer to a physical habit like overeating or smoking or an attitudinal habit like arrogance or vindictiveness. This type of karma can sometimes be changed by insight and willpower. One might realize that he is doing the wrong thing and simply change the unwanted behavior. Of course, one must examine the behavior, decide to change it and motivate oneself to effect the change. Although it may be difficult to do, it can be done. The moment the behavioral change is made, one's future karma is altered. The person who curtails his eating will obviously lose weight. The arrogant person who becomes humbler will have better personal relationships.

Belief Karma

Belief karma is created by our psychological belief system. **We create our reality through our beliefs.** Our thoughts, feelings and attitudes all arise out of the complex belief system we have about ourselves in relation to the world. Our beliefs are constantly changing as we immerse ourselves in the sea of life. However, our most cherished core beliefs remain relatively stable. For example, someone whose core belief is that he is alone and isolated in a hostile world will likely spend much time in severe anxiety and depression without knowing why. At this point, one might ask where we get our beliefs? They are formed out of our experiences, particularly early experiences. The quality of our experience is related to the overall needs of the soul. The soul chooses a set of parents and life conditions that are likely to lead to karmic balance and spiritual growth. For example, a soul may be trying to learn the difficult lesson of forgiveness. Parents may be chosen who will not meet the normal needs for love and attention. A resentful, depressed belief system may be created. This is not a punishment, but a spiritual lesson. The person must realize that he can change his current (depressed, resentful) beliefs by forgiving her parents for their neglect and herself for not being more "lovable." The ultimate spiritual lesson here is forgiveness of the self and others. This forgiveness will aid the psychotherapeutic process of belief change. All true psychotherapy implies belief change.

Here is the process of belief change in psychotherapy: First, there must be an examination of beliefs currently held. Second, the effect of those beliefs on one's current life must be experienced. Third, the reasons for developing these beliefs should be explored and re-experienced. This usually includes some exploration of childhood and might include some past life exploration through hypnosis or a spiritual healer. Fourth, the belief in question should be re-evaluated for current appropriateness. A belief held at age twenty may be outmoded by age forty. Fifth, the emotions connected with the belief should be experienced again and released.

Once the decision is made to let go of the old, negative, outmoded belief, it can be replaced by a positive belief. Creative visualization can be helpful here. This visualization will be especially helpful if the new belief is more in line with universal love than the old one was. For example, a belief that one is alone and isolated in a hostile world can be replaced by belief that one is connected with all others in a world geared toward love and growth. This change would be immensely beneficial. Most belief changes, however, are smaller than this example. This is due to the resistance to changing deeply-held convictions and beliefs about life. People frequently tell me that bad things keep happening to them! I reply, "That is because you are clinging to negative beliefs!" I firmly believe, however, that a motivated individual can change his beliefs and hence his karmic fate. All psychotherapists are actually helping their patients change their karma. The positive effects will be felt in this life, as well as future lives.

Destiny Karma

Destiny Karma consists of certain things which cannot be changed in this life. For example, a person born with only one arm is not going to grow a new arm. However, the quality of his current, one-armed life and the karmic implications for future lives depend on his attitude toward the affliction. If he is angry and bitter about his fate, he will create more bad karma. If he is philosophical and uses the one-armed life well, no more bad karma is being created and his current life becomes happier.

The important points to remember are these: The soul is continually trying to grow from life to life. The spiritual growth can be imagined as a shift from negativity to positivity. Another way of saying this is a shift from selfishness and material values to selflessness and spiritual values. Does this process sound familiar? It is a core belief of this book. The process of change unfolds according to the law of karma. As the person gradually realizes that she is reaping what she planted earlier, she decides to plant new and better seeds in the form of better beliefs. Understanding and working with karma aids in this essential switch.

In psychotherapy, the emphasis remains on what can be done in this life to make it better and happier. However, by opening up the vista to include the influence of past lives on the current life, motivation to change can be increased. The patient can now deal with and take responsibility for changing beliefs and change his karma. The new and better attitude now becomes, "What am I waiting for? I will use all experiences learned in this life as well as previous lives to create a better reality now. I will work with and through the law of karma to create a great reality. I will heal myself and contribute to universal healing!"

CHAPTER 22

The Power of Prayer Revisited

As the author of two books on psychotherapy and healing, I sometimes reflect on how I got my firm belief in the power of prayer. Then I remember my father, Victor Menahem, and his firm belief in prayer. Victor was the editor of the Bulletin for the *Jewish Center of Bayside Oaks* in Bayside Queens. Here is what he wrote in an editorial printed in 1965:

> My dear friends, we come to the synagogue for two reasons: to thank God for the blessings received and to pray for the accomplishment of wishes most desirable to us. Prayer, and particularly communal prayer, is a most formidable instrument. To be effective, prayer must originate in our hearts and be sent out through our mouths by all the will power at our command. Our surroundings must be calm, free from distracting noises, foreign threats and the like. These only create a field of static, which distorts and dilutes the strength of our prayers, thus rendering them inadequate in the accomplishment of their aims.
>
> If you cannot follow the rabbi in Hebrew, there is always the English text; failing that, you may pray silently from within, but always fervently, fully confident that GOD HAS

THE POWER and HE WILL GRANT WHAT YOU ASK FOR!

Follow these simple thoughts and you will be amazed at the results you can achieve.

Well written, dad! One of his favorite expressions was that "the apple doesn't fall far from the tree." So understanding of metaphysics helps us switch from material values to spiritual values. Then, prayer, from the heart, helps us further to make the switch.

Can prayer be studied scientifically?

In 2006, a review of the scientific studies on prayer was released that suggested that prayer is not really very effective. Many of my skeptical friends brought it to my attention. "What do you think?" they asked. They were really probing me to see if I had finally come to my senses and give up on this God and prayer stuff. Of course, it did nothing of the kind. This chapter is my answer to research, and an update of my ideas on prayer and healing.

I was trained as a psychologist in the 1970s. I liked psychoanalysis, especially the ideas of Karen Horney, M.D. I thought that if I was completely analyzed, a la Horney, that I would be completely mentally healthy. I had been exposed to some New Age thought in my training, but I thought psychoanalysis was the answer. I did not consider religion and prayer as relevant to my life or the therapy I conducted with patients.

As I entered the 1980s, the New Age Material was gaining ground. Psychoanalysis wasn't enough for me. I practiced transcendental meditation and read The Seth Material, which said that we "create our own reality" as part of "All That Is" (God). Thus, my new concept of God was that we are all God (not to be confused with the ego). However, prayer is not addressed in this philosophy. Rather, releasing negative beliefs and affirming positive beliefs to replace them was suggested. We are told in *The Nature of Personal Reality* by Jane Roberts (the previously mentioned "Seth" author) that we "are much more than we think we are." In other words, we are more than just bodies with egos. This was an integration of body mind and spirit, but I did not really see it as spiritual. I saw it as psychological. There was some change in my therapeutic outlook, but it did not include prayer.

In the late 1980s I faced a personal crisis, initiated by the suicidal patient I discussed in chapter three. After that experience, I began to research prayer and started writing a new book, later published in 1995 as *When Therapy Isn't Enough: The Healing Power of Prayer and Psychotherapy*. I began to pray for my patients. I sometimes prayed with my patients. I suggested they pray for themselves. I learned through my research that, according to Aldous Huxley, in his book "The Perennial Philosophy," there are four different types of prayer; petition, intercession, adoration and meditation. I saw that prayer was not to be used to get external "things." Rather, prayer was for character change, asking God for guidance and strength in changing what needs to be changed for psychological and even physical healing. The petitions became thankful affirmations. For example, I would say "Thank you God for healing the roots of my discomfort or illness." "Thank you for healing (fill in name) for the highest good of all concerned." The prayer is the same for oneself or someone else. Soon I realized that even prayers of adoring God were helpful. The personal will and its "vibrations" were then in accord with God's will. This tends to produce healing.

The same is true of meditation. Meditation is entering the stillness of God, the gap between thoughts and staying in this silent gap, with no attempt to cajole God. It has a healing function. God knows what to do. This is where I was in the 1990s. I found excellent results with my patients; many were helped by a combination of prayer and psychotherapy. The scientific studies, of Dr. Randolph Byrd seemed to confirm my experience. I noticed that prayer and meditation helped people with a wide variety of anxiety and depressive disorders. Even physical ailments tended to get better faster than expected. I remember once praying for my daughter, who was overseas, in Israel, and was feeling flu-like symptoms. She called the next day, completely better.

As the twenty-first century dawned, I knew that prayer was very helpful in healing, due to my need for healing. I continued with affirmative prayers for healing on all levels. Nevertheless, I had a variety of physical symptoms, including shortness of breath, anxiety, gastrointestinal symptoms and pain. I believe I spent entirely too much time evaluating and obsessing about my physical symptoms. I had to find some way of letting go of the obsessive negative thoughts about heart problems and death. I needed a new perspective, something to take me beyond the physical body. My own great cosmic lesson plan required letting go of self-pity and developing a new way of looking at the world. Even my manner and understanding of prayer needed a revamping. I found that using the words "I am" was necessary for the effectiveness of the prayer. Remember God's response to Moses as to who sent him to Pharoh. "Tell him 'I am' sent you." Once, when having difficulty breathing, I began to affirm "I am breathing freely and easily. After about 5-10 minutes, my breathing eased. I created a daily prayer: "I am happy, healthy, peaceful and strong, thank you God" I repeated it endlessly and started to feel better.

I also began to practice the 365 lessons from *A Course in Miracles*. Each lesson is an affirmative prayer to be used all day long. One lesson is: "I am as God created me, his son" (we are all his sons and daughters). On this day I felt so good I could hardly believe it! I believe that these prayers work on healing the mind and body. It is not just forgiveness at a behavioral level, but a true joining with God in prayer that leads to a forgiving attitude. This is the healing. The forgiving attitude leads to the switch from a body/ego dominated life to a spiritual life. All the research focuses on healing the body. Hence, they miss the main point of healing through prayer. The body will last as long as it is necessary to make as much spiritual progress as one can in this life.

I believe that affirmative prayer can help us heal. However, we are not supposed to use prayer as magic to heal physical symptoms. There has to be a real attitudinal healing and understanding of God and our relationship to God. If God is our source, we are actually still part of God. Thus, we are not really even in relationship, we are part of the Oneness. The nature of that oneness is love, peace, kindness and joy. Forgiveness is the path to realizing and experiencing this good.

Recent prayer research has a fundamental flaw. The well- intentioned researchers are looking at prayer as a magical physical healing technique. They are looking to a powerful sky God, separate from us, to see if he can heal the alleged "real problem," physical symptoms. The only measure of the prayers "working" to empirical prayer researchers is physical healing. Might there not be other measures? What about a person who dies more peacefully than he would have without the prayer? What about the person who simply lasts longer than expected? What about the possibility that the sick person had just finished his life and did not need to go on living?

Prayer is much more than just a magical technique for symptom relief. It is a movement toward holistic healing of the entire human being. I do not believe that this can be measured scientifically. It can only be experienced holistically. A person knows when he is being healed. He can sense the changes in a spiritual orientation to life. The prayers become affirmations of what lies beneath the turmoil of the usual physical reality. Thus, I can only continue to affirm healing for myself and my patients and friends, becoming a beneficial healing presence to anyone I encounter. I cannot presume to know what is good for anyone else. That is up to the other people with whom we are connected in God. That is all anyone can do. We must use prayer to deepen our understanding of the spiritual nature of life, making the spiritual cognitive shift, experiencing deep peace This will result in many healings, some spiritual, some psychological, some physical. Sometimes it will seem that God said "no" to the prayers. Actually, it means that physical healing was not right at that time in the way we think of it. In the end, our bodies all die, but if we die with spiritual vision and enlightenment, they have been worthwhile.

CHAPTER 23

When Bad Things Happen... A Response to Rabbi Harold Kushner

In 1981, Rabbi Harold Kushner published a runaway, best-selling book, *When Bad Things Happen to Good People*. Rabbi Kushner, who had just suffered the tragic loss of his fourteen-year-old son to a devastating disease, progeria, was naturally grieving deeply. His loss tested him to examine his faith and beliefs about God. He asked a deep and profound question. How could a loving, omnipotent God allow so many bad things to happen to so many good people? Many people feel they are being punished for some unknown misdeed when bad things occur. Other people conclude that there is no God. Still others search for some meaning in their misfortune. They get angry at God for what happened but agree to accept it only if they can discover a reason why a loving, all powerful God, would want something terrible to happen to them. Rabbi Kushner, clearly a compassionate man devoted to the welfare of others, wrote his book to reconcile his tragic loss with his faith in God. His conclusions clearly made sense to many people.

The Story of Job

Through examining source materials like the book of Job, he concluded that many people's understanding of God is inaccurate. In order to explain his understanding of God and life, the Rabbi reviews all the unhelpful responses of Job's well-intentioned friends. Essentially, Job was a very good man who lost his family, possessions and health, because God made a wager with Satan. God bet Satan that Job would remain faithful, no matter what happened. Satan said Job would curse God when things went wrong. Some of Job's friends tell him he must have done something bad to deserve so many bad things happening to him. Job knows that he didn't do anything wrong and does not deserve punishment. He was a pious man. His friends tell him to examine his life again. Nobody is perfect and he must have done something wrong. Job gets really angry at his friends and insists that he is a good man, better than most. The friends decide that he is arrogant in his assertions and that is why he is being punished.

"God is good, fair and just," explain his friends. "You must retain your faith," they insist. Job gets even angrier, insisting that he is innocent and shouldn't be punished. Finally, Job turns to God himself with his anger. God then appears in a whirlwind, and rebukes Job, essentially telling him that when Job creates a world, as God did, then he can challenge God. God wants Job to become humble and accept his fate. God has a wider perspective on things than any human. Job finally concludes that he must accept what happens and make the best of it. When Job makes this fateful decision to retain his faith, God rewards Job's faith and humility with the return of his material health and wealth, and gives him a new family to replace the one he lost. The message is essentially one of faith and humility. We are being instructed to step back and admit God knows better than we do. We should be pious, and pray for the strength to make the best of what we have, even if we are bewildered, angry and grieving. This is an excellent teaching story.

After much thought, study of texts like the story of Job and emotional processing, Rabbi Kushner reaches his own conclusions about God, how the universe works and how to deal with tragic events. "God is good" says the Rabbi, "but he does not control everything." He is not a God who rewards good deeds and punishes bad ones. He created a world that is basically good and harmonious. The sun always rises in the East and Sets in the West. There is beauty everywhere and many people are good. Yes, bad things happen, even to good people. But mostly, the world is good. So far, I agree with the rabbi. However, he concludes that **bad things happen for no reason at all. (In my opinion-incorrect)** *Rabbi Kushner thinks that* bad things in one's life may have no ultimate meaning. They just happen. That is all. Despite our personal tragedies, says the rabbi, we have to retain our faith, become angry if we feel angry, feel our grief and respond as positively as we can. We must create our own meaning out of the chaos. We should not encourage others to "get over it" quickly and move on. People often feel a lot of angst, and must be allowed to feel badly as long as they need to. (I agree) We should not encourage grieving or suffering people to look for some ultimate spiritual lesson, says Rabbi Kushner. Now, I agree with Rabbi Kushner that grieving people must have time to grieve and be angry. You can't rush anyone into looking for meaning in loss. However, I disagree with the Rabbi's conclusion that we can never find any meaning in loss because the events of life are random and meaningless. In fact, the worse the events that happen to us, the more we should look for their meaningfulness!

He feels that there is no spiritual lesson in tragic loss. We should simply pray to God for the strength to live with tragedy. Kushner asserts, since God is loving, not mean or punishing, He will then provide the strength for us to keep living a good life. Perhaps then we can create our own meaning from events. God does not create tragedies to teach us anything. Rabbi Kushner feels that only, a mean, cruel God would create pain and suffering to teach a spiritual lesson. God is not mean and doesn't want people to suffer. He is just there to offer strength and comfort when we suffer from outrageous fortune. This is a different understanding of God than most people have. For Rabbi Kushner, God is not omnipotent in the sense of changing events to protect good people. God's omnipotence is the ability to give strength and comfort when approached via prayer. I agree with these assertions. But I disagree that God isn't trying to teach us anything. God is trying to teach us-that is the great cosmic lesson plan.

Who is Responsible for Bad Things?

When I first read this book, in the early 1980's I didn't find it very helpful and wondered why so many people loved it. I was more of a New Age person. I believed that we create our own reality, through our beliefs. God, for me, was more of a nonjudgmental energy source. My first clue to the popularity of Rabbi Kushner's philosophy was the title. Everyone thinks they are good and are being treated unfairly when bad things happen. Some people conclude that they are being punished for some unknown misdeed. Others conclude that there is no God. Rabbi Kushner's appeal is related to his creative synthesis of these two positions.

According to the Rabbi, there is a God, but God does not dictate what happens in the world. Neither are we personally responsible for the bad things that happen to us. Rabbi Kushner's belief is that we didn't necessarily do anything wrong when bad things happen. We are not being punished. Thus, *no one is responsible for bad things.* No guilt for you and I, no guilt for God. *Bad things happen for no reason.* We are off the hook. God is off the hook. But, and this is a big but, there is a God and he is a powerful source of love and comfort. If you pray to God for strength, you will get it. You will survive, like Job. Thus, life is more good than bad. It may seem unfair at times. But hang in there. That is Rabbi Kushner's theory. Nobody is guilty, nobody is to blame, bad stuff just happens. Life is essentially random. Yet, there is a powerful God, who can give us strength, but does not make the bad things happen. Rabbi Kushner's message is to have faith that we can receive help from a loving God, but don't expect magic.

To this day, I disagree with this theological point of view. I agree with the Rabbi that there is a God of some sort. I agree that God does not make things happen to punish people. I agree that God loves us and provides comfort. But I strongly disagree that things happen randomly. I believe that,

Everything happens for a reason!

We just don't know the reason is sometimes. If we pray, ask for help, strength and guidance, our still small voice inside will help us find a spiritual lesson. As, Dr. Frankl often said, "Life must have meaning." And bad things are part of the learning. Yes, we suffer, but not because God is punishing us. I agree with Rabbi Kushner here, but I think God is teaching us something and some of the lessons are painful. Dr. Frankl, a concentration camp survivor, said he found meaning by helping the other prisoners in Auschwitz and keeping notes for his future book, *Man's Search for Meaning.* For Dr. Frankl and I, life is a "great cosmic lesson plan."

I have concluded, after many life experiences, that God is trying to teach us something. We, as human beings, are very resistant to learning it, just as almost every patient is resistant to getting well in therapy. For psychotherapy patients, the problem is usually unworthiness, which is primarily unconscious. I believe this unworthiness or unconscious guilt is a universal problem that is rarely recognized without help. After forty years as a psychotherapist, I have some tentative answers to answer the question of *why* things happen and what we need to learn.

God, in the previously mentioned "Seth Material" is called "All That Is." Human beings are much more than we think we are. We are "multi-dimensional beings," existing on many levels. We are a part of "All That Is." Each human gradually develops a belief system, which then manifests within physical reality. There are also group beliefs that manifest via the law of attraction. Thus, God or "All That Is" does not haphazardly or cruelly make bad things happen to us. Rather, we are **co-creators** of our reality. God provides the energy or medium within which we have beliefs and tend to attract other similar beings to create a reality where anything can happen. Seemingly random events can be explained as co-creations of human beings who need to expand their horizons beyond the conscious ego, within the multi-dimensional "Allness," God. This is reiterating the law of attraction I had learned in the Robert Collier material (The Secret of the Ages-1926). Our learned negative beliefs tend to attract negative events. This is how the lesson plan works. When we begin to upgrade our beliefs and attract better events and people we can see our part in the creation of our lives. Eventually, we can reach the point of experiencing God's love and Oneness and accept what happens. We can change what we can change and accept the rest.

The "good" things, we don't question. The so-called "bad" things we don't like. We don't feel we deserve bad treatment, because we are (consciously) good. So we blame God, bad luck or randomness. Most people have no concept of anything to be learned (God's lesson plan). Nor do they have any concept of the input of our own beliefs or emotions (the law of attraction). That is seen as blaming the victim. In recent years, the idea of God's plan has prospered in some (mainly Christian) philosophies. The idea of personal creation is popular among new age believers. That philosophy promises much more control over events than when God was simply causing everything.

The New Age promise, exemplified in the Seth philosophy, is to simply change your beliefs and get what you want. What I am suggesting here is that a synthesis of Western religious and New Age philosophies makes the most sense. It is not only God's will that is being enacted here. God is a totally loving consciousness. "His" only wish is for all of us to wake up and join him in this loving, peaceful, non-judgmental state of being. *That is the lesson plan*. Nor are events simplistically created by our negative beliefs. Both points of view have some validity. God wants us to be more loving. But our negative beliefs, *most of which are unconscious*, take us in another direction, helplessness. That is why many people want an all-powerful God to control everything, prevent bad things from happening and essentially bail us out. In my model of the universe, everyone is responsible. God wants a variety of things to happen until we learn to be more loving, kind and peaceful. We need to own our own power to change beliefs as much as possible, toward the way God wants them. *We need to accept our power to change what we can change, as well as our inability to change and control everything.* In the mean- time we suffer. We resist responsibility until we learn to change what we can change and accept God's will-the lesson plan.

When we have limiting or negative beliefs, powered by fear, anger and guilt, some "bad" things are bound to happen. It is inevitable, that is the human condition. Imagine a world in which everyone got what they wanted, right away. Imagine a world in which nobody ever got sick or died. It would get pretty crowded here. This is not saying that we "want" tragedy, illness or loss. However, within physical reality, everyone dies and people often get sick. Illnesses are related to many factors, ranging from heredity and pollution to stress (related to negative beliefs) and pathogens. Death, although it is a tragic loss to us on the human level, is primarily a change in focus to the spiritual plane. The soul or spirit is now focused on another plane-without a body.

We, the physically living, are so focused on our body we cannot see that there are other levels of reality. Jewish doctrine supports the existence of an eternal soul, which will be resurrected at the end of days. The Jewish Kabbalist doctrine of "gilgul" supports the ideas of reincarnation and karma, as do Hindu and Buddhist religions. Jewish Kabbalists believe that there is existence beyond the physical being that we know. It is puzzling that these doctrines are so rarely utilized and accepted by Westerners. Though I agree with Rabbi Kushner that these doctrines would not help people suffering from the early stages of grief and mourning, they would in the long run help us progress in life.

The Stages of Belief

I believe that Judaism is correct in asserting that all humans are born with original goodness. Babies are shining with joy, goodness and energy, until the harshness of the separation-individuation process (growing up) happens. We then realize that we are at the mercy of our caregivers. We are likely to feel "alone and isolated in a hostile world." Even, with loving, caring parents, who set good limits, we have to grow up and find a way to survive and prosper in the physical world. In order to do this, we are almost inevitably cut off from our Spiritual source so that we can survive as a set of beliefs, an ego in a physical body. Most of us believe that we are conscious ego (our beliefs, created out of experience), living in a body. To the extent we believe in God, "He" is an old man, in the sky, with no body, controlling and creating our lives. That is the traditional view of God, taught to children by the Western religions. Allegedly God is all good and all powerful. If we are good, we will be rewarded. If we are bad, we will be punished. The bad things are the punishment. This makes God into Santa Claus. Yet, many people retain this view all their lives. I call this the first stage of God belief.

The second stage of God belief is that there is no God. Thus, everything is random. Kushner has a unique synthesis of these two concepts of God. He accepts randomness of events-but he also posits a powerful God to help us cope. He seems to push for God as a source of love and comfort, who does not intervene in the world or cause bad things to happen.

On the other hand, there is the metaphysical view of God is an energy that embraces all there is. Humans are co-creators of physical reality with God, through their belief systems. Taken, naively, this creates a system of philosophy where we are "ego-inflated." In other words, we think that if just think positively and exude love and peace all the time, we can control everything and make only good things happen. Unfortunately, due to the inevitable traumas of being human, we do not feel good and happy all the time. For some people, this new age belief system works for a while...until something really bad happens, like an illness we cannot control or a major loss through death or destruction. Then, we either blame God, randomness or ourselves for thinking negatively or having negative beliefs. Blaming ourselves and thinking we can fix everything with a positive attitude is sometimes called the "spiritual bypass." The spiritual bypass posits that we can control and eliminate all pain and bad events by just thinking positively. This leads to New Age guilt. In this ego-inflated state, some of these New Age people might even blame others for getting sick or creating bad things.

This is the third stage of God belief, "I can control everything by simply changing my thought and beliefs." Stage three takes a truth too far. We are more powerful than we think we are, but we cannot control everything by being spiritual. Thinking we can control everything ourselves is not helpful or called for, especially when people are grieving. Critics of the

New Age like Rabbi Kushner, claim that their "ego inflated" cohorts are "blaming the victim." Actually, I believe that even victims are just people learning, sometimes in a very difficult way, about the wonderful creative process called life, through their beliefs, conscious and unconscious. Seth encourages us to view life as a "playful experiment." Our beliefs are powered by emotions, conscious and unconscious. As human beings, we need to become aware of our beliefs, connect them with our emotions and experiences, and gradually upgrade our beliefs. As our belief systems upgrade, we naturally align ourselves with goodness, kindness, love, peacefulness and other spiritual values, as well as the familiar New Age "abundance." But (and this is a big but) nobody can control everything so well that nothing bad ever happens. There are always some residual negative beliefs and emotions. We just have to keep learning, growing and becoming better, more spiritual people. The lesson plan is that we are co-creating our lives with God. Yet, we need to retain humility and recognize our oneness with the ultimate source of being, God.

Steps to Healing and Enlightenment

Rabbi Kushner's philosophy, I believe, is an attempt to help people live and have faith, despite seemingly unfair events in their lives. As a man of immense faith, a helper, a rabbi, he could not blame God for his personal tragedy. He also could not see that any personal beliefs or emotions could ever have anything to do in any way, with the metaphysical creation of events. In a personal letter to me, he strenuously objected to new age philosophy. In his writings, the Rabbi had to say that no one is responsible for what happens. At least it made people feel better than if they thought God was punishing them for being bad. In actuality, *everybody is responsible for what happens.* It is supposed to be that way, and it is too bad that it usually requires suffering to get to the point of spiritual insight.

Oneness is the fourth stage of understanding G-d. We are one with our creator. To sum it up, we are *co-creators, with the Godly energy,* of physical reality. Our contribution to the equation of why things happen is our beliefs, glued in by emotions. We are individual manifestations of divine energy, endlessly creative on the physical and well as other levels. If we are all part of the same whole, there is no point to selfishness or narcissism. We can drop our belief that we are alone and isolated in a hostile world, run by an uncaring God, or no God at all —just randomness. Once we realize that we are all connected and part of the same Oneness, we can work toward bettering the conditions of being for all human beings. This is the great lesson plan, a *"spiritual cognitive shift!"* We can simply use our unique talents and abilities to better our lives and the lives of those around us. Cooperation becomes more important than competition. The inevitable suffering entailed as we get to the big shift in how we think, is a complex result of the interplay of our beliefs and emotions and the emotions of those we attract to us to learn our spiritual lessons together.

God does not create the bad things that happen to people. However, we are not simply creating bad things by ourselves. There is a co-creative process, which leads us to true spirituality.

God does know better than us. There is a great cosmic lesson plan. We must tune into it. God has no limiting beliefs as human beings must inevitably have. God doesn't need a belief system. He knows how things really are, fantastic! We must act and take whatever control we do have of situations. We must take responsibility for our thoughts, feelings and emotions. Also, we must pray to God for the strength and courage to become unselfish, cooperative, loving and kind toward our fellows and planet. We must let go of anger, fear, guilt and negative beliefs continuously. We must work on upgrading our belief systems on an ongoing basis. My motto is:

Let go! Let go, let God! Accept healing!

Human beings and God create lives together. Pray, as if that is all that is required of us. Take action as if there is no such thing as prayer.

123

Take responsibility to do what we can do, control what we can control and turn the rest of our life over to the divine source, the Oneness. This turning over process is the non-attachment that Buddhists talk about. As Dr. Thomas Hora said, "Yes is good. No is also good." As we let go of our negative, limiting beliefs, let go of our attachments to what we consider positive outcomes, we become more and more aware of the love that binds us all together. As anger, fear and guilt gradually subside, we become aware of the loving Oneness that is our true selfhood. There are many paths to this love. Waking up to the love that is requires the willingness to engage in a lifelong process. The path may include self-searching, therapy, prayer, meditation or even listening to certain popular songs.

As the Beatles sang at the end of the Abbey Road album:

"And in the end, the love you take…
is equal to the love you make."

CHAPTER 24

Non-Judgmental Awareness-
Is it Possible or Desirable?

Part of spiritual healing is the development of non-judgmental awareness, a way of thinking that leads to healing body, mind and spirit. At first glance, the idea of becoming non-judgmental seems like a utopian fantasy. How can we not exercise good judgment in our everyday affairs? Isn't it important to weigh things carefully and make good decisions? Shouldn't we be careful about who we associate with? Shouldn't we delete e-mails promising us a great deal of money with little effort? Shouldn't we look both ways before we cross a busy street? Shouldn't we fight against war, poverty and injustice?

Obviously, when we use the term, "non-judgmental," we are not talking about doing things that are injurious to ourselves and others. We have to use "judgment" to take care of our physical being and those close to us. What I am really talking about here is the desire to look at ourselves without presuming that we did a wrong or bad thing. Of course, we must take responsibility for our own decisions. We can change any decision we make, without condemning ourselves. Otherwise we fall victim to emotions like self-hate and depression. I call it the "shoulda-coulda-woulda" syndrome. In other words, I "should" have done things differently, so I am an idiot for making bad or self-destructive decisions.

Judging Others

The situation gets even worse when we judge others. Now we are directing our judgment outward, leading to anger. "They" should have done things differently, preferably our way! We know better than "they" do about whatever it is. So we are angry at them. Maybe we even hate them. We have little or no control over them, so we may feel powerless and even angrier. This is the state of many interpersonal relationships and the world at large today. When we judge ourselves, we get depressed. When we judge others, we get angry. Sometimes we get afraid of retaliation from those we are judging. We call this anxiety. Around and around we go, feeling guilty, angry and fearful.

As judgmental individuals, we keep therapists busy. Also, the big drug companies are happy to sell us tranquilizers and anti-depressants. So perhaps judgment is good for the economy. On a global basis, judgment leads to huge problems like violence, terrorism and war. Political leaders say that "my" country is better than "yours." If you disagree with me, my country may threaten to invade and conquer you. " This is the kind of judgment we need to avoid. Maybe a lot of judging isn't as good as we think it is. Perhaps, no matter how smart or right we think we are, we need to step back and allow differences in others. Perhaps the beginning of non-judgmental consciousness is tolerant behavior. Tolerance of other people and other ways can only help people get along better. Do we need to go any farther? I think so. Is it really possible or even desirable to walk around this crazy world thinking that everyone is O.K. Perhaps the field of psychotherapy can lead the way in this area.

Client-Centered Therapy

Back in the 1950s, Carl Rogers created a new type of psychotherapy. He called it "client centered" therapy. He felt that the client-centered therapist should be totally open to the patient and his problems. The ideal client-centered therapist was supposed to be genuine, non-judgmental and cultivate unconditional positive regard for patients. These qualities of a good psychotherapist are generally well accepted now, no matter what theoretical orientation is followed. An open-hearted, compassionate therapist accepts his or her patients as they are. He or she is non-judgmental! This enables the patient to heal, become happier, more peaceful and more positive in life. In other words, the "Rogerian " oriented therapist is modeling non-judgmental behavior for the client. If the client internalizes this attitude, he or she feels better and heals. If this is true in psychotherapy, wouldn't it be a good idea for the general population? We could begin with tolerance of others and work our way toward not judging others. Judgment could be eliminated by compassion. We could also accept our own decisions and accept ourselves the way *we* are. Sounds like a good idea, does it not? But how could we cultivate such an attitude without putting everyone in psychotherapy?

Perhaps a clue lies in meditation and contemplation. At the simplest level, we could learn how to be aware of our thoughts and feelings. We could see how judgment leads to anger, fear and guilt. We could see the seeds of aggressive or violent behavior before we explode. Once we see that the enemy is within us, we could become aware that as we let go of all the judgments, especially the ones attached to negative actions. We could feel a sense of peace inside ourselves. With practice, we could even sense a peace or spiritual presence in others. Maybe we could realize that negative behavior of others is due to their fear, anger and guilt. We could learn to respond to others with compassion. We could accept them as troubled, rather than stupid or evil. *A Course in Miracles* says that all human behavior is either an expression of love or a call for love. Perhaps non-judgmental behavior on our part can help others heal. Perhaps compassion works better than correction. We could spend most of our time expressing love.

We all have a tendency to judge. In working with my own judgmental attitudes, I developed a new prayer. With great humility, I wrote this prayer for myself and anyone who could benefit from the new spiritual lingo to a very old prayer. Christians will recognize it as a re-write of the "Lord's prayer." Here it is.

One source of all Being, hallowed be thy essence.

Thy kingdom come, thy will **IS** done,

On Earth, and in the world of spirit.

Give us this day, our daily sustenance.

And forgive our errors and we forgive the errors of others that seem to hurt us.

And lead us not into the temptation to judge, criticize and condemn ourselves or others.

And deliver us from the evil of holding onto fear, anger and guilt.

For thou art peace, and love, kindness, compassion, gratitude, forgiveness, joy and wisdom,

Forever, amen!

My personal practice is to repeat this to myself each evening, before bed. Then, when I catch myself judging during the day, I consciously let go and follow the wisdom of the Beatles, "Let it Be." I invite any readers that are interested to develop their own practice in non-judgmental awareness. I think it is a good idea.

John Flynn is a wonderful singer/songwriter. He wrote a fantastic song, "I Will Not Fear," following 9/11 to help people combat the fear and judgment that grew out of that attack. Basically he was writing about facing our own demise with grace and courage. I re-wrote the lyrics to help myself and others who may face death from my aforementioned illness. If we can get the idea that we are more than just "a body" we will be better able to face existential fear, fear of our own mortality. Giving up all negative judgment of ourselves and others can help us face all fear.

CHAPTER 25

I Will Not Fear

Sung to the music of "I Will Not Fear" music and original lyrics by John Flynn

The doc takes out his stethoscope,
and listens with his ears.
He says I might need surgery.
That brings me close to tears.
I know I had a heart attack,
But it's been several years.
So I simply tell him, "Doc,"
"I will not fear."

I will not fear, I will not fear. Say it in a voice that's loud and clear
Sing it out for all the world to hear, I will not fear, I will not fear.
I feel my breath is getting short,
So I prick up my ears
I try to take a deep long breath,
It seems like death is near.
I think about the ER now,
Is 9.1.1 time here?
But I gather up my strength
And say "I will not fear."

Repeat Chorus

My field it is psychology
I have a Ph.D.
I know a lot about the mind,
And what it does to me.
Yes, it can make my body hurt
Or even disappear,
Then I remember what I really am,
And say "I will not fear..."

Repeat chorus

CHAPTER 26

A Poem to Heal By

As a poet and a songwriter, I wrote this poem to help me heal after my heart attack:

Life is but a waking dream,
It isn't really what it seems.
Solid matter, flesh and bones,
are really formed by light and tones.
Things in all their density,
flowers, trees, you and me.
Infinite duality,
When all the while,
Beneath the molecule dance,
We're in a funky,
profound, trance.
Pain seems so real,
And so does fear,
In desperate times we shed a tear.
When all the while, deep inside,
A tiny spark of spirit hides,
Waiting for the proper moment,
psychic revolution to foment.

Enlightenment comes to thee,
We're floating in a cosmic sea,
There's nothing there for us to see,
Just an end to duality!

Unity, Oneness, Love and Peace,
Worldly conflict will not cease,
But the inner eye can now see,
The inner truth that makes us free!

10/18/03

CHAPTER 27

Guided and Unguided Meditation

We've talked about the importance of prayer and contemplation. Let's get down to practicality. What is the best way to meditate? Should we just sit and breathe? Say a mantra? Get hypnotized? Listen to music? Let's explore.

My introduction to meditation was learning "clinically standardized meditation," a variation of Transcendental Meditation, developed by Patricia Carrington Ph.D. in her 1978 book, "Freedom in Meditation." She gave us a choice of mantras. We were told to pick the one that appealed to us. I picked, "sat yam." We were told that the mantras had no particular meaning (though I later learned that "sat yam" means truth). All we had to do is repeat the mantra silently for twenty minutes. Eventually, we would automatically shift into a peaceful, almost blank state of mind. I found this practice very soothing and practiced on and off for years. This form of unguided meditation was heavily promoted as a "technique" for relaxation.

This was especially true after the research of Herbert Benson at Harvard. Dr. Benson instructed his subjects to repeat the word, "one" internally for twenty minutes. This form of unguided meditation was found to lessen anxiety, lower blood pressure and lead to a more peaceful life. Later, Benson found that meditation was even more effective if the mantra was meaningful to the meditator. Initially, he thought the word "one," was meaningless. Then, he realized that his initial mantra, "One", actually had meaning on a spiritual level. Indeed, meditation is much more that a technique. I believe it is a method of quieting the chattering ego mind, and becoming one with the greater Cosmic Consciousness or God. In later years I also learned *vipassana,* or insight meditation, with equally good results. Insight meditation consists basically of sitting quietly, being aware of your breathing, and allowing all thoughts and feelings to arise. You don't push away the thoughts feelings and sensations, you just watch them, non-judgmentally.

In addition to practicing non-guided meditation, I learned to practice hypnosis. Some people, myself included, feel that hypnosis can be a sort of guided meditation. During the 1990s I was trained as an Ericksonian hypnotherapist. Milton Erickson, M.D. went way beyond traditional hypnotherapists with his "utilization" method of induction. He utilized the patient's already existing cognitive framework to create an open-minded form of hypnosis. During this trance, the patient could be "guided" to access already existing solutions to chronic problems. The Ericksonian idea is that you know how to solve your problems (unconsciously). The creative unconscious is then is empowered, directly or indirectly, to solve the problem in its own way. The emphasis is on utilization and non-directiveness. When hypnosis is seen in this way, it is very similar to guided meditation.

Traditional hypnosis emphasizes the creation of a dissociated mind, splitting the conscious and unconscious minds. However, when used in a meditative way, the patient is "guided" to contact the one mind, or Higher Self. Contact with the higher self automatically leads to peace of mind. This is the same goal as meditation, reconnecting with the One Mind. The old form of hypnosis implied commanding the problem to be healed. Ericksonian hypnosis, or "guided meditation" does not command anything. It suggests that there is a way to heal and the way includes reconnecting with the one mind, which then solves the "problem" for you. Let go, let God and accept the healing.

It may seem like a great leap from meditation and hypnosis to humor as a part of the great cosmic lesson plan. But the Maharishi Mahesh Yogi was always laughing and so was Dr. Erickson. I believe that developing a good sense of humor about life is essential to the healing process. Thus, I offer the next chapter, the great cosmic chuckle.

CHAPTER 28

The Great Cosmic Chuckle

Did you hear about the two satellite dishes that got married?
The wedding wasn't much…but the reception was great!

How about the Zen monk who walked into a Burger King and said, "Make me one with everything."

Are these "one liners" corny? Perhaps, but they are indicative of my approach to life, as well as the psychotherapy I do.

Some people say I remind them of Groucho Marx. Groucho often said, "That's the most ridiculous thing I ever hoid." Other people say I remind them of the 1970s, funny, Woody Allen. Do I have "the head of a crab and the body of a social worker?" Still others say I remind them of Dr. Sidney Friedman (played by Alan Arbus) of MASH. I do look a little like Alan Arbus, but, actually, I think it is my humorous attitude toward life they are picking up. I simply believe that one of the reasons we are here on Earth is to have a good time and I will do anything (well almost anything) to promote a spiritually high sense of humor and well- being in my patients, friends and relatives. To me, "enlightenment" means lightening up. According to Dr. Hora the purpose of life is to be a "beneficial presence." Humor is a vital element in living the kind of positive life we are supposed to live. God wants us to be happy. I intend to obey that law.

When I think about it, I have always integrated humor into the therapy I do. As a young therapist, I would throw "one liners" out in diagnostic interviews. If the person didn't at least smile, I assumed they were depressed (it couldn't just be a bad joke). Perhaps my comical nature was infectious (joculitis?) Anyway, even in my early years as a therapist, I couldn't pass up opportunities for jokes. A patient suffering from phlebitis would be asked how he got inflammation of the "FLUB." I would often tell humorous stories and repeat plots from ancient sitcoms. I was not just going for cheap laughs, but searching for therapeutic metaphors.

For example, I might say, "Did you ever see the Sgt. Bilko episode where he stopped his scheming and became nice?" Before long, all the troops wonder "What's wrong with Bilko?" They want the old Bilko back." This is, of course, a good story to tell anyone who is having trouble accepting themselves (in other words, most people). The message is simple, be yourself, people will usually accept you anyway. There are many such messages in the old sitcoms. They are untapped goldmines of therapeutic metaphors.

In an earlier chapter, I discussed the case of Harry in relation to Buddhism and meditation. Here, I would like to mention the power of humor to help him heal his depression.

Despite the pain he suffered, he had a good sense of the absurd. As we spoke of his parents he began to feel their pain and see that they were clueless as to what they were doing to him. I jokingly called them "bozos". He loved the appellation, and never called them anything but the "bozos" again. Somehow, just using that name helped him to see the humor amidst the tragedy of his dysfunctional family. Harry has come a long way in working through his feelings about his dysfunctional parents. They were more lovable as "the bozos" than as just mom and dad.

On another occasion, Harry and I were discussing the importance of changing one's beliefs and perceptions. He was insisting that he couldn't "see" things any differently. He thought that he was always going to be alone and miserable because of his parents mistreatment of him. I tried many therapeutic metaphors to stimulate forgiveness and change, including the experiment where people adjusted to prism lenses that made everything appear to be upside down at first, until their eyes adjusted. This metaphor did not click, until I did something odd. I said I could help him see things differently without saying another word. "How?" he challenged. At this point, I just reached over and put his glasses upside down. He broke up with laughter and felt significant relief of his depression for the following week. He actually reported that he was looking at things differently. Even a year later, he reported that he sometimes breaks a depressive mood by putting his glasses on upside down.

Harry is, by profession, an environmental engineer. He helps maintain clean water for all of us. Of course, the most famous sewer worker of all time is Ed Norton of The Honeymooners. Harry even mentioned that they had once given out "Norton" T-shirts at an office party. Once it was established that he liked Norton, "Honeymooners therapy" was started. Frequently, I will begin a session with him by stretching out my arms (a la Norton) on the famous $99,000 Dollar challenge episode of The Honeymooners. On that particular episode, Kramden's response to Norton's arm stretching was to scream at Norton to cut it out and get to work, playing the piano, so Kramden could test himself on his knowledge of pop songs.

One day, Harry walked in with a long face, I just stretched out my arms like Norton, getting ready to play the piano. Harry laughed uproariously and said, "Damn it, I wanted to be depressed and you ruined it." I had humorously broken the "depressive trance" without saying a word.

It has been easy since then to use many Honeymooners themes in his therapy. Most often, it is to establish a humorous perspective to the current situation. Gleason's writers' were geniuses. They got Ralph into all sorts of schemes to make a lot of money. This is the American way of being successful. Of course, every scheme backfired, since no scheme can succeed when you believe in scarcity and unworthiness as Ralph Kramden did. Ralph's schemes to make money never worked, but more importantly, he did realize that he was lucky to have a great wife like

Alice and a great friend like Norton. This was a brilliant switching of value systems. I am sure that Dr. Hora and his group approved. The importance of love and friendship over money is a significant reframing of life values for many people. Somehow, it has more impact when presented in a humorous, indirect way, than if it were just stated. Referring to this classic TV show is a great teaching device for switching from materialistic values to more spiritual ones.

Don's Story

Another client came in complaining of depression. Don was a perfectionist who couldn't stand it when things went wrong at work. Since he was a New York City guidance counselor, things frequently went wrong. He often reacted by getting more depressed. I searched for a way to get him to lighten up. Suddenly, I had an image, William Bendix in "The Life of Riley. " TV show.

I said something like:

Me: Do you remember the Life of Riley TV Show?

Don: Sure, with William Bendix.

Me: Right. Do you remember what he said when things went wrong?

Don: (after a moments-thought) "Yeah…What a revoltin' development this is?"

Me: Right. And how might this this apply to you?

Don: What do you mean?

Me: How about saying that phrase to yourself when anything goes wrong.

Don: O.K.

This statement was extremely helpful to him on many occasions. Pattern interruption had worked again, fueled by humor.

My Friend Mack

In addition to sitcom characters, I utilize humorous real characters from my life. One of them was my army buddy, Robert McCary (Mack). He was a happy fellow who didn't let much bother him. If he saw me feeling down, he'd ask what the matter was. No matter what I said he waved his arm back and forth and said, "Don't mean nothin, don't even mean nothin..." I'd usually laugh and my angry or depressed mood would be broken.

The other day, while looking for ways to help still another depressed client break the spell, I thought of Mack. The client, a small, pretty 40 year old woman made quite a contrast to the Mack in my memory (a muscular, bearded African-American man). The contrast in their stature seemed funny to me. I told her about Mack and how he'd wave his hand and say his line. A week later, she came in waving her hand and reported that she been using it all week and it worked great! We both laughed as she waved her hand and said..."don't mean nothing...." She reported that this humorous technique helped her often.

My Groucho Glasses

In addition to helping alleviate depression, humor works just as well with fears, phobias and anxiety. I was working with one fellow, Jack, who had agoraphobia with spontaneous panic attacks. The primary treatment was to drive with him as far as he could go (a technique called "in vivo desensitization"). He gradually became desensitized to the fear and could go much further than when the therapy began. As he reached his limit, he would pull over and take a few moments to calm down before continuing.

In searching for a way for him to make further progress, I suddenly realized that he couldn't be laughing and afraid at the same time. I knew that an important element of humor is surprise. So I hit upon the idea of slipping on Groucho glasses when he was too busy panicking to be aware of his surroundings. I hid the glasses in my pocket and waited until he started to panic. He pulled over, as usual, whereupon I put the Groucho glasses on and called his name. He turned, looked at me, had a startled look on his face and then cracked up. His fear immediately subsided, and we were able to drive further from his home than ever before. He then asked me if he could drive with "the Grouchos" on and proceeded to drive confidently, and asked me if he could keep the glasses. I agreed and he kept them in his glove compartment in case he needed a humorous interruption for his panic.

The Genius of Seinfeld

I find that Seinfeld is perhaps the best, most therapeutic comedy written since the Honeymooners. It is a gold mine for psychotherapy. The most helpful episode was the one where George Costanza does everything backwards. Jerry suggests this move, asserting that since everything George does turns out wrong, if he did the opposite, everything would go right. Thus, George boldly goes up to an attractive woman and says, "I'm unemployed, broke and live with my parents. Would you like to go out with me?" The girl agrees. Later in the episode he also gets his dream job with the New York Yankees, by confronting their fiery owner George Steinbrenner. After Costanza insults Steinbrenner, the owner says calmly, "hire that man."

I have used this episode numerous times in therapy. However, the case of Marco stands out in my mind. Marco was a chronically depressed, angry middle-aged man. He would constantly lament that he had made many bad moves in his life. Thus, he had never gotten what he wanted to get out of his life. At age, 62, he was "running out of runway." Seizing my opportunity, I asked him if he had watched Seinfeld. He was familiar with the show, so I reminded him of the "Do everything backwards" episode. He liked the idea and began to put it into operation. His life immediately improved. He got the job he wanted, resumed dating and quoted George to me. Like George Marco once said, "This isn't a technique, it is a religion." He had finally grasped the concept of the importance of beliefs in creating one's life. His low self-esteem had sabotaged success. By merely acting "as if" things would work out by doing the opposite, things did work out. By doing the opposite, he was assuming things would work, and he was right. All this was done lightheartedly, inspired by Seinfeld (a fellow graduate of Queens College-CUNY by the way).

I used the same episode with another patient, James. I simply asked James which Seinfeld character he was most like. Again, it was George, This time, I suggested he switch to Kramer. He found this so helpful that he leaves each session moving his arm like Kramer, saying "giddy up!" He signs all his e mails, J. Kramer and Associates. His diagnosis is bipolar disorder. This is also my diagnosis of the "George" character. George goes back and forth between rage and depression, which is one form of bipolar disorder. The difference is that James has gotten much happier and more stabilized and has been stable for some time now.

The Lion Tamer

Joke-telling is an art with much therapeutic potential. Beyond the laughter, there can be much truth to a joke. One of my favorites was often told by my uncle Sol and concerns a lion tamer. An old lion tamer is showing a trainee how to do it. "First," he says, "you hold the whip in your hand and the chair in the other. Then, you whip the lion and keep him at bay, any questions?" "Yeah", says the younger man, "what happens if the lion kicks the whip out of your hand?" "That's easy", says the experienced one, "just use the chair, pick up the whip and continue." "But what if he kicks the chair out of my hand?" "Also simple, just use the whip, pick up the chair and continue." "But what if the lion kicks both the whip and the chair out of my hands?" "That's also easy" says the old man, "just reach behind you, grab some s--t, throw it in his face, and blind him," "But where will I get the s--t?" The older man says, ***Don't worry, it'll be there.***

This joke almost always gets a laugh. But, more importantly, it teaches the listener that when you need immediate help, you just reach deep inside you and the answer will automatically appear. Without getting preachy, the joke suggests unconscious or spiritual resources that will be there when you need help. It combines laughter, metaphor and indirect suggestion. One client who was told the joke in his first session still finds it valuable, years later.

It should be clear by now that there are infinite ways of using humor as an aid in the therapeutic process. It can be utilized as a pattern interruption, direct suggestion, indirect suggestion, teaching tale, or general mood elevator. But I believe that humor and laughter should not be confined to formal psychotherapy. I see it as a highly evolved way of looking at life, applicable to everyone.

Is Humor a Spiritual Thing?

Sigmund Freud, father of psychoanalytic therapy wrote a book entitled, *Jokes and their Relation to the Unconscious.* The theory of this book is that jokes were always sexual or aggressive in nature. This idea coincided with his view of the unconscious mind. Jokes, for Freud, were simply a way to express unconscious sexual or aggressive feelings, in a socially acceptable way. But I propose a new theory of humor and its relation to human life. I believe that humor is a key element in reaching enlightenment. Approaching life as an often-funny "cosmic chuckle" can transform sorrow and depression into a creative learning experience.

In the Western world, we are taught from earliest childhood the importance of success, competition, getting ahead and being financially independent. We make lots of plans, expecting happiness. But, as John Lennon said, "life is what happens to you while you are busy making plans." The ability to step above the plans, laugh at ourselves and our fellow humans and relax, can turn depression and anxiety into peace and contentment. The unconscious mind is much more than a hotbed of sex, aggression and repressed traumas. It is cosmic consciousness, waiting to burst forth in the form of humor. Humor is a very spiritual way of looking at life. I have showed how classic sitcoms, jokes, props, and the element of surprise are all part of the spiritual psychotherapy I practice. My fervent hope is that more psychotherapists pick up the baton of humor and make it part of the spiritual healing of their clients.

I hope it is becoming clear that I take a very light approach to life and enlightenment. When I teach my class in non-traditional psychotherapy at Teacher's College, Columbia University, I do one session on Humor and Music in psychotherapy. This is usually the most popular of all the sessions of my class. I believe that it is because humor, a lighter approach to therapy and life helps us enormously in coping with the thing called life. I have seen quite a few spiritual teachers in my lifelong search. Every one of them has had a great sense of humor. At some point in life we have to let go, let God and enlighten up-laugh at ourselves.

I am aware of the "heavy duty" philosophy presented in this book. Thus, I hit upon the idea of presenting this philosophy in a much lighter way. Thus, the next section of this book will illustrate the importance of enlightening up. It is a fictional romp toward enlightenment, through the eyes of Dr. Hans Off, a chiropractor who gets bitten by an aardvark, in Davenport, Iowa. Unable to pursue his specialty, chiropractic, he becomes a psychoanalyst. Unfortunately, he develops a harrowing psychological problem. He begins to hear voices. Thus, he naturally seeks out his own analyst to cure the problem. This novelette is a romp through the four forces of psychotherapy. Analytic psychotherapists assume that voices are split off projections of a sick and fragile psyche. Much of the time this is right. But what about the cases where the voices are positive and trying to guide the person? Many psychics, healers and mediums claim to hear positive voices and successfully help a lot of people. I have been to many psychics and healers and have been helped through difficult times. Read on to find out what Hans Off's voices teach him about psychology, spirituality and life!

PART TWO

Hans Off: The Psychologist

CHAPTER 1

Hans Off Begins his Great Cosmic Lesson Plan

"Psssst, Off." There it was again, the voice. Dr. Hans Off had been hearing that voice for more than two months, but he could not get used to it. His training as a clinical psychologist led him to think that he was in the midst of a nervous breakdown. Mentally, he ran down the criteria for diagnosis. Were the voices auditory hallucinations? Yes, he was hearing this voice. Flattened affect? Well, he had been a little depressed lately. Autistic thought process? Well, he had been daydreaming more than usual. Loose associations? True, his thoughts had always been loose. In fact he prided himself on this fact. These four "A"s, to diagnose schizophrenia had been proposed by Dr. Eugene Bleuler in the nineteenth century, when schizophrenia was called "dementia praecox." Nobody used that term anymore. The common word was schizophrenia. Off began to worry that he was a schizophrenic. "I worry, therefore I am," thought Off, paraphrasing philosopher Rene Descartes. Before he could go into one of his philosophical tangents, more evidence of schizophrenia? Tangential thought?, the voice returned.

"Psst, Off."

"All right," muttered the psychologist, "what is it?"

The voice now assumed a regal air, something it seemed to do when Off would finally acknowledge its existence.

"I want to help you."

"How can you possibly help me? You are a disembodied voice, a split off projection of my repressed, ego alien, shadow self."

"You are wrong, Jung breath."

Not only was this hallucination annoying, it was arrogant and very knowledgeable.

"O.K., smart ass, who are you? Carl Jung? Albert Einstein?"

"You humans are so "dense." You have so much to learn. You think spirit guides are mere figments of the imagination. Then, if you finally wake up a little bit, you want a spirit guide that was a famous person. Almost never do you realize that helpful spirits are not necessarily famous souls. Now do you want to know who I am?"

"I'm afraid to ask." muttered Off. "O.K., who are you?

"I am Dr. George Groddek!"

"Will you get to the point" demanded Off!.

Suddenly he realized he was arguing out loud with an auditory hallucination, claiming to be the soul of a pioneer psychoanalyst that had been forgotten by time! He wished the voice would let up, but it persisted.

"I want to help you with your existential dilemma."

Off had always been troubled by the great existential problems; death, meaning, responsibility and freedom.

"O.K Dr. G. Which one of the great problems do you want to help me with today?"

Off scoffed at the inner voice."None of them."

The inner voice continued anyway," Today I just want you to acknowledge that I am not a mere hallucination. You are conversing with me, are you not? I am your spiritual guide!"

Off realized that whatever he was talking to, there was some conversation going on. Who the heck was Dr. George Groddek ? These answers would have to wait for another day. For at that moment the phone rang.

"Hello, Hans, it's me...."

Off hated it when people said "It's me." All this meant is that it wasn't Off himself, a fact he already knew, despite his impaired mental status.

"And who are you? Off replied, in an offhand manner.

"Hansie, it's me, Bella, Bella Donna."

"Oy Vey," thought Off. All I need today is the melodrama of Bella Donna. Despite his annoyance, he replied in his usual cheerful tone, "Hey Bella, what's shakin' ace?"

"Now, that sounds more like my favorite shrink, listen, I need a favor." A favor, Bella always needed a favor.

"O.K." what sort of mess are you in now?"

"Well, nothing big, I just got arrested, and I need someone to bail me out. Nobody down here at the jail believes me, so I need someone who can convince them I'm not a lunatic. You believe me don't you?

"Of course I do. What kind of psychologist would I be if I didn't believe my patients say to them . Now, what is it that I should believe?"

"Well, it's why I got arrested."

"O.K.," "Why did you get arrested?"

"Well, I didn't mean to do anything wrong. I didn't even realize what I was doing anything wrong until the fuzz arrested me." Off could hardly wait for the latest misadventure of his flakiest patient. Bella looked like a cross between Janis Joplin and Scott Joplin. Come to think of it, nobody knew what Scott Joplin looked like, nobody except Off, who had studied ragtime music with Scott in Joplin Missouri.

"Hans, are you listening?"

"Oh yeah, sorry just thinking about ragtime music....so how did you get arrested, Bella?

"Well, I was standing on the corner of Walk and Don't Walk..."

"Bella, that's not a corner, that's a pedestrian crossing sign.

"It is????"

"Yes, so what did you do?"

"I hailed a cab."

"You got arrested for hailing a cab?"

"Yes, in my birthday suit."

"You hailed a cab in the nude?"

"No the cabdriver was properly dressed, I was naked."

"And why were you naked?"

"It was hot."

"You got naked in the middle of New York City because you were warm?"

"Yes, is there anything wrong with being comfortable?"

"No"...

"I thought you always told me to be comfortable with myself"

"I did but...."

"Well then, what's wrong with what I did? I was only doing what you said...then the cab driver stares at my tits, can you believe that...So I told him to put his eyes back in his head and take me to Tiffany's."

"Tiffany's???"

"Yes, it was nine A.M. and I wanted to have breakfast."

"Breakfast ? Sure, don't they have breakfast at Tiffany's anymore?"

"Bella!!!! You got into a cab naked and asked the driver to take you to Tiffany's for breakfast?"

"Yeah, and this asshole has the nerve to drive right past Tiffany's, drive me downtown and tells me to get off at Blueview Hospital."

"So you got out?"

"Yeah, but I refused to pay the whole fare and he had me arrested. Now will you please come down to the station and bail me out?"

"O.K. but it may take me a while to get enough cotton."

"Cotton?"

"Sure, to" bale" you out."

"Dr. Off, that's bail, not "bale." Just bring money for bail."

"Oh, in that case, I'll be right down."

Off ran downstairs and hailed a cab. He wasn't the least bit surprised that his driver was named Mary. Things like that always happened to Dr. Hans Off.

Safely ensconced in his New York City Taxicab, he looked more carefully at Mary's hack license. "Mary Magga Di Lena" he read aloud. Sounded familiar but he couldn't place it. Perhaps it was an Italian bakery in his old neighborhood. Or maybe it was a girl he had a crush on in the sixth grade. He couldn't be sure. Off was so lost in thought that he was startled by the mellifluous voice of the cabbie.

"Where to? well-dressed Jew?"

"How did you know I was Jewish?"

"Aren't you Dr. Hans Off?"

"Yes, do I know you?"

"No, but I saw you on Oprah last week."

Off couldn't believe how many people had seen him on Oprah. It was amazing how many people were interested in chiropractors who became psychologists.

"So what did you think of the show?"

"It was O.K., but not as good as Tibetan gurus who work in delicatessens: Are they really Deli Lamas?"

Off tried to think of a clever reply, but all he could think now, was that he had to get downtown and bail out Bella.

"Thirty third and third" said Off, hoping his Brooklyn accent was gone.

Mary Magga Di Lena skillfully weaved her cab through the dense traffic and pulled up in front of the fifteenth precinct. Or, as the police themselves called it, the old one five. After paying the fare and giving her a good tip (don't play the stock market), Off hurried inside to find a frantic Bella, sitting at the desk of a haggard looking old detective that reminded Off of the meatballs he had for dinner last night.

"What is your name, officer?"

"Meatball" replied the weary policeman. Off wasn't surprised, things like that were always happening to him. Jung explained it with his theory of synchronicity. These events were somehow connected though in a non-causal manner. It was more than a coincidence that this man reminded Off of a meatball and was also named Meatball. Once again, reality forced Off to interrupt his reverie.

"Do you know this woman, Doctor....?"

"Off, Dr. Hans Off, Yes, she is a patient."

"Well doc, we got some pretty serious charges here, indecent exposure, theft of services, disturbing the piece."

"That's disturbing the <u>peace</u>" interjected Off, peering at the charges in written form.

"Whatever" answered, meatball "Do you have the bail?"

"Just one cotton pickin' minute"

Meatball thought he was going to scream, another bozo making bail jokes.

"Just pay the clerk" demanded Meatball, calling to his clerk.

"Hey, Yoyo, take care of this guy, will you."

"Wait a minute" interrupted Off, Is his name really Yoyo?"

"Yes, why do you know him?"

Do I know him? Of Course I know him. He's a toy that goes up and down..."

"Blarney, we have another head case here."

"Wait a minute officer. Do you mean to tell me that your captain is named Blarney Stone."

"Yes"

"And I suppose you have some leprechauns too."

"Yes..."

"Oy mein Gott, I really am in another world. What is going on here? First I hear voices. Then I slip into an alternate reality composed of fictional characters who think they are real."

Off did not know what was real anymore. Was subjectivity objective? Or was objectivity subjective? If a tree fell in a forest with nobody there to hear the sound, would it make a sound? Was Heisenberg right that there was always an effect when an observer entered a system? Who was observing this lunatic scene composed partially of real characters like himself and Bella and partially of fictional characters. "Who am I?" thought Off.

Suddenly he felt his body shaking. Bella was shaking him so hard he could no longer introspect.

"Hans, Hans, wake up! You have to bail me out of here."

Still in a stuporous state, the dubious doctor walked over to the one called "Yoyo" and gave him the bail. Grabbing her doctor by the arm, Bella whisked Hans to the street and took a deep breath.

"Whew, I thought I'd never get out of there."

Hans was slowly returning to his usual state of consciousness.

He quickly decided to postpone any further metaphysical questioning and deal with the immediate situation, Bella Donna on thirty third and third.

As soon as Bella realized that her doctor had composed himself, she launched into her usual litany of semi-paranoid delusions.

"Hans, why were those cops staring at me? I didn't do anything wrong. I just wanted to assert my rights as a citizen."

"Were you naked when they brought you in Bella?"

"Yes...but..."

"That's why they were staring at you."

"Big deal, you'd think they never saw a beautiful naked girl before."

"Bella, men stare at naked women, they always did, they probably always will."

"Well, I don't like it, they shouldn't do that."

"Next time, wear clothes and they won't stare"

Off was pleased by his courageous confrontation of his "borderline" patient. According to Dr. James Masterson, authority on borderline patients, one had to confront the self-destructive behavior in this type of unstable, explosive patient. The confrontation had to be done with compassion, in such a way that they could tell the doctor had their best interests at heart. Once they grasped the futility of the self- destructive habit, they could drop it and become self-enhancing.

Off waited for a reply to his therapeutic intervention. He got one soon enough.

"F--k you Hans, eat s--t and die."

"Did I offend you Bella?"

"No, I always tell people I like to perform unnatural acts and eat excrement."

Aha, sarcasm, thought Off, another defense of her fragile ego.

"Bella, its O.K to be angry and sarcastic with me, but who did you get angry with earlier in your life?" Now Off was going for a complete psychoanalytic, genetic interpretation. If she could see that she was repeating a maladaptive style developed in childhood, she could learn to change it.

"You remind me of my uncle Arnie Killarnie."

"Uncle Arnie?" This was a new twist. Usually they were angry with a parent. But perhaps she was close with this uncle. "Tell me about your uncle Arnie, was he Irish?" asked Off, suddenly aware that he was still on a crowded New York street.

"Well, actually no." replied Bella, "he was from Irkutsk."

"Did you say your ear hurts?" he interjected

"NO!" said Bella, I said he was from Irkutsk..."

"So he was an Irkutstian" answered Off.

"Yes replied Bella, what difference does it make?

"Well, in psychoanalytic school, they taught us to watch out for orthodox Irkustians...Only Freudians were acceptable."

Just thinking about Freud took Off back to his graduate school daze. Off had always been prone to spontaneous trance states. He would be lost in thought, appearing dazed to those around him. Actually, he was in a creative, alpha state which he found more stimulating than his immediate sensory environment. Jung would have called him an intuitive-feeling type. That is, Off processed information through his intuitive function, grasping things as a whole, without knowing exactly how he knew what he knew. Most of his friends were of the opposite type, sensation-thinking. They reached conclusions via evidence from their five senses and their thoughts. Neither type could fully understand the other. But the sensate types always had a good time at the expense of the intuitive types. In his boyhood Vienna, Off was known as "dummkopf". In his adolescence in Brooklyn of the 1960's, he was known as the #1 space cadet of Ocean Parkway.

His tendency toward reverie made him frequently forget appointments. This day, starting with Bella Donna's plea for help at nine A.M., was no exception. Before he could properly delve into the actual existence of Bella's alleged "uncle Arnie Killarnie, from Irkutsk," he remembered his appointment with his own analyst, the eminent Otto B. Anal, M.D., Ph.D. L.S.M.F.T. (Lonely Short Man Fond of Tortoises). Off didn't really know what LSMFT stood for, but Dr. Anal did have an aquarium filled with turtles in his office. Plus, he wore tortoise shell glasses. Anyway, Off had to leave Bella at thirty- third and third to get to Dr. Anal's Office on sixty sixth and sixth. Otto hated it when his patients were late. He considered it a personal insult to arrive late at the office of the founder of F.A.R.T. (Freudian Analysts Rigorously Trained). Off was quite aware of the pedagogic predilections of his analyst. Dr. Otto B. Anal certainly fulfilled the stereotype of the so called "anal triad" (thrifty, orderly and obstinate). He was cheap, neat, and stubborn and Off did not want to cross him. Unfortunately for Off, his next cab driver was not nearly as deft as Mary Magga di Lena. Of course, he looked at the hack license, but the name Slim Goslow didn't seem significant at that moment. Though Off had never before had a cab driver who asked him what a yellow light meant.

"Slow Down" Off replied reflexively.

"Okey Doke" muttered the driver, as Off squirmed and looked at his watch. The big hand was on the twelve and the little hand on the eleven. It's going to be close, thought Off, as they pulled up to the immaculate tower containing the office of Dr. Otto B. Anal, The Babylonian Society and the Home for Retired Curmudgeons. Dr. Anal once told him (in a rare violation of the blank screen rule) that he yearned to be a Babylonian curmudgeon and had picked this building because of the proximity of the other tenants.

Off paid the fare and raced past the doorman, and up the stairs. Huffing and puffing, he entered the waiting room just in time to hear the toilet flushing. Dr. Anal had just finished his morning meditation (practiced on the throne, of course) pondering whether he was anal retentive or anal expulsive. Dr. Fritz Perls would have called this type of exercise "elephant shit." But to Dr. Otto B. Anal, it was serious business.

CHAPTER 2

....

Hans and Otto

As Anal peeked out into the waiting room, he asked the usual question. "Vas ist Los?" (What's happening) to which Off replied (as usual) "Der Hund ist los." (The dog is loose) This exchange had gone on twice a week for twelve years. Though Off was getting a bit sick of it, he knew his mentor loved it and didn't want to disappoint him.

Thus, after once again stating that the proverbial dog was loose, Off lied down on the couch and began producing his usual mish mash of "loose associations." This was the golden rule of psychoanalysis. Say whatever comes to your mind, no matter how trivial or silly it may seem. Eventually, it will lead to a therapeutic cure. A "transference neurosis" will develop, wherein the analyst will be distorted in the image of a significant figure from the past. For example, if the patient had a critical mother, the silent analyst would soon be seen as being inwardly critical. All of the early wounds of the narcissistic period of childhood would them be exposed, aired out, worked through, and cured. In the example above, the patient would eventually realize that everyone was not as critical as his mother. This would help him have happier relationships. All the patient had to do was talk, about anything, and eventually she would be cured.

Off was eager to please his analyst and spent many hours talking about his alleged happy childhood in Vienna. He had lived at Bergasse 17. By coincidence it was next door to the home and office of Sigmund

Freud. Freud himself was long gone when Off was born in 1947. But Off was always fascinated by the continual stream of people coming to see what had become a museum. Like Freud, Off was interested in healing. Off, however, became interested in the chiropractic method and had left his Vienna of sacher torts and apple strudel for the Center of the chiropractic world, Davenport Iowa. If not for a freak accident, Off might have stayed a chiropractor. However, shortly after receiving his degree, Off was bitten by a rabid aardvark.

Nobody could ever remember seeing an aardvark or anteater of any kind in Davenport. But things like that were always happening to Hans Off. He was later to build a theory on all these strange events. His conclusion was that *"everything happens for a reason. "* That reason is the psychological and spiritual growth of the individual person and the species homo- sapiens. In other words, we are here for a" great cosmic lesson plan." He would later feel that we should strive to understand the encoded messages of life events. If we refused to listen, more and more suffering would be administered until we got the message: Develop a high degree of "menchiosity." Be the best person you can be. Learn to love God, yourself and all other people you meet.

In the Davenport of 1969, however, Off was extremely pissed at being bitten by the only aardvark ever seen in Iowa. Despite receiving the series of painful rabies shots, his right hand was paralyzed, making him a rather impotent chiropractor. Clearly, he thought, "my life is ruined." He pondered returning to Vienna and becoming a CPA (He was to call the store, Hans Off Cleaning, Pressing, Alterations). His father had been that type of CPA but Hans wanted more. He wanted to be a healer. At the time, Off leaped out of his chair (a davenport, of course) and shouted "I'm going to be a headshrinker."

Off began his meanderings on this day by ruing his decision of 1969. "I don't know why I became a headshrinker. Every day I work with flakes like Bella Donna. Some of the older flakes have white hair. I call them "frosted flakes." Kellogg's makes the best frosted flakes. But that blonde bombshell Bella Donna is some flaky babe. Can you imagine, I apply perfect psychoanalytic technique, gently confronting her self-destructive behavior, and she tells me to eat s--t and die. Where is the gratitude?"

"You want gratitude?????" interjected Anal.

Off hesitated. He didn't know the correct answer. He didn't know what his beloved Dr. Anal wanted. Then he remembered the golden rule and just continued his associations.

"Darn straight Dr. A. When I help someone, I want them to praise me love me and tell me I'm brilliant."

"Und how long have you had this narcissistic delusion Dr. Off?"

Now Off was really upset. His doctor thought he was paranoid, with delusions of grandeur, just for wanting some gratitude?"

"I am not paranoid"

"Are so."

"Am not"

"Are so"

"Am not"

"Choose you, odds one."

"O.K."

"Once, twice three shoot, mine, no penny tax no nothings. You are so paranoid Hans."

Once again Hans Off was defeated by the intellectual superiority of Dr. Otto B. Anal. Was it family therapist Jay Haley who said that psychoanalysis was like a game? The analyst starts out in the one up position. He knows he is superior and so does the patient. Gradually, it dawns on the patient that he is the equal, maybe even superior of the analyst. At this moment, the analyst terminates therapy, remaining one up.

Otto B. Anal was grinning smugly. He looked sort of like the Cheshire cat, right after mating season. He had had his fun for the moment and now it was time for serious business. What did Mickey Mantle hit in 1956? Off hated it when Anal tested him on his obsession with baseball history. ".353" snorted Off, annoyed. "Why do you test me on this stuff?"

"Just feeding your basic narcissism, Hans."

"Is this guy patronizing or what?" thought Off. But all he could say was, "All right, ask me anything, about anything. Anal loved a challenge like this.

"What were the names of the two generals of the imaginary armies in Don Quixote?" Without missing a beat, Off replied, "Alifanfaron and Pentapolin." Anal knew that he was right, though nobody else on Earth would. "That's why I like you Hans, such a good knowledge of important things."

Was this another put down? Off wasn't sure. The only thing he was sure of was that he had to go pee.

Dr. Anal did not like urethral interruptions, but he reluctantly let Off go to the bathroom. As Off relieved himself, his inner voices returned. "Psst, Off," it said as usual.

"What is it?" he inquired.

"Why don't you tell him about me?" That was a good question. Off was troubled by the voices but was reluctant to tell his orthodox analyst about them.

"I can't, not yet, he'll think I'm crazy."

"Tough nuggies" answered the voice. "I want him to know."

"Maybe next time" answered Off, zipping up his fly....

"Owwww..." he howled as his penis got caught. Things like that were always happening to Hans Off. He returned to Dr. Anal's office.

"My penis hurts," said Off returning to his associations.

"Now we are getting somewhere Off, tell me more."

"I just caught it in my zipper."

"Things like that are always happening to you, Off."

The rest of the session was not too eventful.

Anal, aware of his frequent interventions earlier in the session, decided to be silent while Off meandered about from his painful tool to the indignity of working with hysterical drug addicts like Bella Donna.

When the hour ended, precisely at eleven forty- five (therapeutic hours had long since shrunk to forty five minutes), Off bid his doctor farewell in the usual way:

"It's been crazy, Otto." He knew that Dr. Anal hated it, but he couldn't resist the reference to the 1950s instrumental song by that name.

As Off hit the street, he prayed for a cab with an anonymous driver to take him to his office. Off was not surprised when his driver turned out to be Albert Nonamous. Things like that were always happening to Hans Off.

"Ninety ninth and ninth, and step on it."

Off did not want to be late for his next patient, who was new.

CHAPTER 3

Studley Megabucks

Off raced up the stairs and hurried into his cluttered office. He didn't notice the faint smell of cigar smoke or the picture of Groucho Marx that had fallen on the floor. Heart pounding, he looked at the name in his appointment book. The name sounded familiar, Studley Megabucks.

It was happening again. He was being inundated by fictional characters. This character had appeared in an obscure psychology book by a Dr. Sam Menahem, *All Your Prayers Are Answered*. Shakily, Off walked out to the waiting room. "Good morning Mr. Megabucks, how do you do?"

"Just call me Studley, doctor, and I'm rather upset."

"Won't you come in?"

Off settled into his standard issue therapist chair. It was brown leather, with matching ottoman (get it otto-man). Mr. Megabucks sat in the matching brown leather chair and launched into his tale of woe.

"You see, doctor, It's my bank balance that I'm worried about..."

Off cringed at this remark. Everyone always seemed to be worried about money. Off began to think that he had another anal retentive patient, but waited for further evidence.

"You see, the market tanked yesterday and I had a panic attack!"

Off knew Studley had enough to eat, so he tried another form of therapy-asking obvious questions which leads to a logical conclusion. Do

161

you have "what to eat?" asked Dr. Off in his best Jewish grandma voice. Of course," answered Megabucks.

"Well then, can you pay the rent?

"What rent?" answered Megabucks, "I own three huge homes, all paid for, in New York, San Diego and Irkutsk."

"Do you owe any money?" asked Off.

"Of course not! I have a retirement plan with two hundred million in securities but it went down to $199,000,000 yesterday!.

"I'm so sorry" said Off, pretending compassion. "So what do you think this money represents to you?"

"Are you kidding? "It keeps me safe," said Megabucks." Off knew it was a hoarding impulse, based on early childhood feelings of emotional deprivation and fear. But what he said was:

"Take two aspirins and call me in the morning." Then he added a behavioral technique, which Dr. Anal would have heartily disagreed with.

"Stop" he shouted, utilizing a technique from behavior therapy designed to stop obsessive thoughts. It also worked well at busy intersections.

Studley Megabucks immediately stopped whining and sat up straight in his chair. He promised to use the "stop technique" and follow his doctor's orders. Off then free-associated to his patient about the reason for his panic about money. The words came out of Off's mouth, but it seemed as if he was channeling another source, perhaps that voice who had assailed him earlier. The inner voice that came out of Off's mouth spoke forcefully, "You see Mr. Megabucks, many people have more money than they need and then use it to make more and more while other people who don't have enough are thinking of ways to grab it from the guys who are piling it up."

"But, isn't it human nature to be greedy and driven by the desire to get more stuff and live bigger and better?"

"I can see how you would think that. But from this vantage point it is perfectly obvious that the greed arises out of distorted beliefs and emotional problems."

"So why is almost everyone greedy and driven down here?" asked Megabucks.

"People incarnate on Earth in order to learn to be more giving, caring loving and spiritual in general," Off opined.

Off liked his little rant, but wondered privately why almost everyone is so screwed up, even rich people like Mr. Megabucks." To his own surprise, against all psychoanalytic rules, Off continued his rant.

"Earth is a remedial planet, where only the slowest learners and worst cases get sent. However, the spiritual impulse is there and can't be stamped out. Look at the Soviet Union. The communists tried to stamp out God and ended up in total ruin. The state is not God, but neither is the ego." He continued his speech to Megabucks, "You must maintain your humility if you are to grow. You see, many people on Earth think that they are nothing more than a body with a small amount of awareness they call their ego. They think that anything they do, they do themselves. They are very proud of themselves for being successful and better than other people. That is ego in the negative sense. They have totally lost their connection to the divine, even though it continues to exist in their subconscious mind. At a very deep level, all minds are joined. Dr. Jung told us that. He was one of the first westerners to realize this. The materialistic egotists however, have gotten so far away from their divine source that they don't even think it exists. Once they think they are nothing more than isolated bodies with ego awareness they become terribly afraid. They feel alone and isolated in a hostile world. They see no recourse other than to compete with other egos and try to pile up the most money, hence greed. If they are good at the game, they think that they are God or godlike and can do anything they want. Analysts call these people narcissists. If they are bad at the game, they get angry, say it isn't fair and feel sorry for themselves. Some of them just wallow away their lives in fear and depression, while others feel justified at stealing, killing and all that jazz to try to even things up."

He continued: "They never realize that the only real solution is to change their way of thinking, get themselves a different set of rules. If they realize their connection to God and each other, they will quite naturally cooperate for the common good. They wouldn't be driven by fear. They would be driven by love. All your major religions actually teach this but few really understand it. It is easy to follow the Ten Commandments when you want to. The eightfold path of Buddhism is easy too. All people have to do is truly understand the spiritual nature of all beings, including themselves and they will stop being greedy and selfish and start working for the common good."

"You make it sound so easy." replied an astonished Studley Megabucks.

"No actually it's quite difficult. That's where I come in."

"What do you mean?"

"I am going to teach you how to wake people up to the truth. Will you cooperate?"

"Wait a minute, cried Megabucks, how did you learn all this? How do I know you're not just a New Age "nut?" "You will have to trust me, have some faith. I am starting a school here teaching psychology and philosophy. It's called the C.L.O.W.N., Conglomerate League of Wise Nutjobs."

"You call yourself a nutjob?"

"Oh yes, I have been learning great humility. I know that I don't know it all, and I laugh about it. You hear cosmic chuckling and guffawing constantly here on this new plane that I have discovered."

"What plane are you on anyway?"

"I am on the plane Jane, in the galaxy of divine jocularity."

"Why did I ask?"

"You asked because you want to know. That is a good quality. Now, will you cooperate or will you cooperate?"

"That's a tough choice. I'll have to think about it."

Off said goodbye to Mr. Megabucks, when he once again heard his inner voice speak.

CHAPTER 4

By George

"I am Dr. George Groddek, the first doctor to treat physical illness with psychoanalysis."

"Holy Munchausen, are you the one who knew Freud?"

"Ja, Ja...he wasn't a bad doctor, though his cigars sure stank."

"What was Freud really like?"

"He was like neurotic, like obsessive-compulsive, like depressed. He did coke, thought it was the cure for depression!"

"What was your specialty, Doctor Groddek?"

"My field of expertise was psychosomatics. I was one of the first to realize that human illness was actually caused by disturbed thought forms and repressed emotions."

"I don't know if I can go along with that."

"Gee, they told me you were an advanced student. Don't tell me you're one of these scientific-materialists ."

"I resemble that remark."

"Ouch, well Off, I won't try to convince you of anything, I'll just continue to summarize what I know, and let you decide for yourself. It was me talking to your patient. You see I developed the concept of the id. I called it, 'das es' which is German for the 'it'. Somehow it got translated as the 'id' in English and was attributed to Freud, who then distorted the concept. The 'it' you see is the sea of consciousness that gives birth to all life. It is invisible and mental emotional in nature.

All individuals, in fact, all life as we know it is a microcosm of the all-powerful stream of consciousness. Most species are totally aware of this truth and just live in harmony with it. The one exception to this is humankind. People are the only species that tend to forget their source. They have this habit of mistaking their tiny bit of awareness for the overall awareness. Once they do that, they get all screwed up. They think that their body and ego is all there is. Of course if this is true, they logically want to protect themselves at all costs. And if they're not protecting themselves, they are busy pursuing momentary pleasures of the body. Most of them never realize that they are "barking up the wrong tree." They don't remember that they are actually lived by the" it." They think they (ego +body) are in charge, when, actually, they are part of the never ending sea of love called the "it."

"That sounds a lot like the New Age stuff I have read about."

"The "New Age" is a misnomer. This is very old stuff, it's just getting a little more popular than it was before."

"But if what you say is true, we should be going in a different direction than we currently are."

"That's right, the human race should be looking for ways to transform their distorted belief patterns into 'gestalts' that are more harmonious with the actual nature of the 'it'...and that's where you come in Dr. Off. We have chosen you to spearhead the consciousness revolution..."

"Get someone else, will you, How about Charles Reich, he wrote a book, *The Greening of America*."

"We know all about Dr. Reich. He made a good start, but he was a sociology professor, a commentator on culture. You are a 'dubledoctor.' You have studied both the mind and the body. By healing people of both mental and physical problems, you can also set them on the path toward higher consciousness."

"How about Ken Wilber, he wrote some really good books on developing consciousness..."

"Wilber is a genius, but few people understand his books. We need a down to earth schlemiel like you to make those concepts understandable to the masses."

"Well..."

"Please....Pretty please...Pretty please with molasses..."

"Oh all right, I feel like Moses in the Bible. I don't see how I am going to get anybody to listen to this New Age spiritual fodder when they could be out copulating and eating out at fancy restaurants. What should I tell them when they ask me how I know all this?"

"Just tell them Groucho sent you."

"What the heck does that mean?"

"Not much, but their puzzlement will make them more open to new answers. Puzzlement provokes an unconscious search for new answers."

"Now that's interesting, where did you get that?"

"Oh, I got it from a man who lived after me, Dr. Milton Erickson. He was a Wisconsin farm boy who learned to become the world's greatest hypnotist after being paralyzed by polio."

"Really? Where is he now?"

"Oh, he has joined us on this side. He's attending the school for spiritual atheists. He's coming along very well."

"Will you tell me more about Dr. Erickson?"

"Sure, we may even invite him here to talk to you some day. He will help you in your task. Meanwhile, just begin to remember to forget all your psychoanalytic psychobabble and tune in to the reality of the 'it.' You are lived by the 'it', whether you know it or not. But it is helpful to know 'it'.

And then, poof, the voice of Dr. George Groddek was gone. Off had actually enjoyed this interlude on the plane Jane. The voice was starting to make some sense, even if it did conflict with the wisdom of Freud, and Otto B. Anal.

The part that scared him was the bit about bringing the spiritual message to the masses. It smacked of messianic thinking. Off had long ago rejected the idea of a messiah, one person saving the world. He thought that if the world were to be saved, it would take the efforts of billions of people, working together.

Yet, there was something to this philosophy propounded by Groddek. He didn't say Off was to save the world, only that he was to spearhead an effort. Leadership he could understand. Thus, he decided to play along with the voices for now, and see where he was led. Anyway, it was time for lunch with his girlfriend, Lola Palooza.

CHAPTER 5

Whatever Lola Wants Lola Getz

Lola Palooza was the most beautiful woman Off had ever laid his eyes (or any other part of his anatomy) on. From the moment he saw her in the Oat Bran section of Whole Foods, he knew he had to have her. He had been so nervous in trying to speak to her that he stammered like Ralph Kramden on "The Honeymooners."

"Homina, homina, homina..." he had said.

And she replied "Is your name Homer, or are you selling hominy grits?"

Instantly, he knew she was the woman for him. Not only was she beautiful, but she had a great sense of Yuma (She was from Arizona). Otto and Lola began to chat over the oat bran. It turned out that Lola was a health food nut. She ate oatmeal for breakfast, tofu for lunch and brown rice for dinner. At that time, Off liked his steak. But the allure of Lola was to lead him in a different direction. Even that first morning, he had found himself eating oatmeal and sipping herbal tea, while ogling Lola. He had never met a Lola before. Though he had seen a movie called the "Sins of Lola Montes." But once he met Lola Palooza, his thoughts were never too far from his libido. In other words, she turned him on, big time.

Lola had a knack of walking in at the perfect moment, and this day was no exception. Just as the Groddek voice had vanished, Lola had burst into his office, wearing the tightest leather miniskirt Off had ever seen on her.

"Hi Hans, Vas ist Los?" (Lola was the only other person that used this expression besides Dr. Anal.)

"Der hund ist Los, Und the miniskirt ist short."

"So, what are you waiting for?"

Hans' member was already standing at attention. Maybe Freud was right, he mused as he unzipped his fly. Perhaps every act was motivated by sexuality or aggression. He could not think of anything on Earth he'd rather do than copulate with Lola. Surely Off was a lucky man. He had a wonderful outlet for his aggressive, sexual appetite. Lola Palooza was as interested in his penis as he was interested in her vagina. In fact, they had pet names for the complementary parts of their anatomies, Pablo and Valerie. Thus, did Pablo enter Valerie. Together, they traveled to the land of Oz and back, carried by the panting moans of delicious sensory pleasure. When it was over, all they could say to each other was. "Homina...Homina...Homina..." Laughing uproariously, they did it again...until there was a knock at the door.

"Who's there?" asked an annoyed Off.

"Orange..."

"Orange who?

"Orange you glad I didn't say banana!" Off did not find this funny, but he opened the door anyway.

"Hey there Hansie boy." said the man in the rumpled hat, T shirt and vest. This was definitely a character. "Hey there Hans, va va va voom."

"Sir, would you please explain your presence in my office?"

"Oh excuse me Doc, don't you remember me. I came in with my buddy. He wanted to get hypnotized to lose weight."

"And what is your name sir?" asked Off.

"Guess," said the man in the rumpled hat.

"Rumplestilskin?" queried the irate doctor.

"Yeah, how did you know?" answered Mr. Rumplestilskin.

"I guessed it by your rumpled hat."

"Well doc, I want to be hypnotized too."

"And what would be your reason for wanting to enter trance?"

"Why that's simple, I want to pass my comprehensive examination in the Philosophy of Existentialism."

Off nearly fell of his chair. "Did you say existentialism, the doctrine that we are defined by our choices and must take responsibility for our decisions in life?"

"That's right Hansie boy."

"You look more like a working man, I thought maybe you worked in a hat factory."

"I did, you are quite a psychic!" Said Mr. Rumplestilskin," but I had to put a lid on that job to go back to school. So I went to the "School for Scary Studies" in Erie Pennsylvania. I became interested in existentialism after receiving my Bachelors' degree. One day, by chance, I was reading the "Classic Comic" version of *"Being and Nothingness"* by John Paul Sartre, when I decided it was my destiny to become a philosopher. You know what they say in the Brooklyn?"

"No, I don't."

"Sometimes a hat is just a hat and nothing but a hat."

Off thought he had heard that before, and realized that Rumplestilskin was paraphrasing Freud. Freud was a cigar addict and was reluctant to submit his addiction to analysis. In his own defensive way, he had rationalized his habit, saying, "Sometimes a cigar is just a cigar and nothing but a cigar."

"Did your friends in the hat factory ever read Freud?" interjected Off

"Nah, most of them were Rankians."

"Oh, Otto Rank?"

"No, doc, rank out-ians, They used to have "rank out sessions," you know, like, "I'll rank you so low you could play handball on the curb, stuff like that."

Off was so confused by this conversation that he decided to drop it. Lola was also annoyed by this coitus- interruptus. Neither of them could determine if this Rumplestilskin character was real or not. But while Hans would always ponder such problems, Lola was more concrete and direct.

"Get outa here" she bellowed, pointing to the door, "Out, out…"

Rumplestilskin scrambled out the door as Hans laughed uproariously.

"Now where were we?"

"We were about to do it again, but I'm afraid we're out of time."

Off sounded like a game show host.

"Can you come back next week and go for the big O?"

Lola giggled, "Off course." Hee hee hee

Lola pulled on her mini skirt and ran out the door.

Hans checked his appointment book to see who his next patient was.

He was hoping for a curvaceous beauty. Instead, he saw the name William Hickock, scrawled in what was apparently his handwriting.

The day was getting worse. Mr. Hickock, of course, was a Sheriff in the Old West. Off peeked out into his waiting room and, sure enough, his next patient was wearing nineteenth-century law enforcement garb, including gun and holster.

CHAPTER 6

Hey Wild Bill

"Hey Bill, come right in" Off said.

His new patient scowled and said, "Please call me Mr. Hickock."

"Okay, Okay, I get the picture," said Off, relieved that at least this historical character was adjusting to the twenty-first century.

"And what brings you here today?"

"Well doc, I can't kill anybody anymore, even bad guys. I am trying to make it as a yoga instructor, teaching the importance of stretching."

"Did you say kvetching?"

No, I said stretching."

"But you were kvetching, that's Yiddish for complaining. You know, slips of the tongue are important."

"Only for hookers during oral sex, doc."

"You are being resistant Mr. Hickok. Why don't you tell me about your interest in sketching, eh?"

"Mister, I don't take well to nosy medicos insinuating that I'm into stuff like sketching. I said stretching"

"Mister Hickok, may I remind you that Dr. Jung wrote of the importance of integrating our latent feminine nature so that we may become whole."

"Feminine, shmeminine, I just want to be able to go back and be a macho sheriff again, I was happy that way."

"Mr. Hickock, may I remind you that you are no longer living in the old west. In 2015 we have laws against this type of thing."

"What do you mean? We are not in the old west?"

"What year is it, Mr. Hickock."

"Why, 1872, of course."

Off panicked. He now realized he was dealing with either a hallucination or a dangerous psychotic. If this man was a figment of his imagination, he, Off, might be mad. If he were real, he, Off, might be dead...soon. Am I mad or dead? (Off thought). He turned it over in his mind, Mad...dead...mad...dead...?

I guess I'm mad, thought Off.

The Hickock hallucination, however, continued to talk.

"Can you help me regain the joy of law enforcement ? Can you doctor?"

Dr. Off decided to confront the problem head on. He would talk to Hickock as if he had somehow skipped ahead more than one hundred years in time.

"Mr. Hickock, I don't know how to break this to you, but the year is 2015." Hickock did not take well to this confrontation. "Don't play with me doc."

"My good man, I don't play games, just look at the calendar on the wall." Hickock whirled to look at the calendar, which indeed said 2015.

"Holy guacamole, I really am in 2015. No wonder I don't feel right. Doc, Doc you gotta help me get back to my own time."

Off was not sure how to deal with this situation. It was not covered in the psychiatric textbook. Nor had he ever seen a seminar on dealing with historical characters who have become displaced in time. Frantically, Off searched his memory for some way of dealing with this confusing situation. His mind raced for something to grasp on to. He could hear his ninth grade math teacher, a certain Mr. Reinfelder, saying, "When in doubt, factor out." Good phrase, but it had nothing to help him with his own doubt. What was factoring out anyway?

Then he heard Davey Crockett say "Be sure you're right, then go ahead." Fine, but how could he be sure he was right. He yearned for a simple rule of thumb, something he could always use in a psychiatric pinch. Then it came to him. Boldly, he turned to Hickock and said, "**How do you feel about living in another time?**"

That was what every therapist said when they had no idea what to do. Usually, the patient would come up with an answer which the therapist could then affirm. "I'm a little upset, but I guess I could click my boots together and say there's no place like home."

"Exactly," intoned Off. "Please pay my receptionist on the way out."

Dr. Off breathed a sigh of relief. That had been a close one. For a moment, he thought Hickock was going to challenge him to a gunfight. But the old sheriff had been pleased with his own advice and had sauntered off to the receptionist. He left so fast that she didn't even get his name.

Meanwhile Off felt exhausted, even though it was only three o'clock. It was not physical tiredness, but the mental fatigue that grows out of a series of insoluble problems. First, Off was hearing voices. Second, he was encountering a series of people that were characters from olden times. These were seemingly monumental problems, indicative of an impending nervous breakdown. Off knew that he should discuss these anxiety provoking events with his analyst. Yet, he was afraid of Dr. Anal's reaction. How could he tell his foremost, esteemed colleague that he was having such problems? Even worse, how could he admit that he kind of liked the voices and found the characters interesting. Off was glad that his four o'clock, Ms. Fifi L'Chapeau had cancelled. Ms. L'chapeau and her hat fetish could not have held his attention long on this day. Off settled back in his standard issue therapist chair and immediately fell into a sleep of frenzied rapid eye movements.

CHAPTER 7

....

The Dream

Off dreamed he was driving a red Ferrari down into the Grand Canyon. He was passing people riding burros with great ease. He was laughing as he yelled things at each burro rider. He yelled, "Get a horse" and "so long sucker" as he accelerated around each curve. Suddenly the Ferrari took off (into the air) and headed for the planet Pluto (the planet Goofy was too crowded). In three seconds, he landed on Pluto and was immediately surrounded by cheering throngs of creatures which were a cross between gastroenterologists and trance -channelers. They had large forefingers like gastroenterologists and large heads like the channelers. Some were able to perform rectal examinations metaphysically.

The leader of these Gastrologers approached Off with great reverence, "Welcome, oh great leader-we have been waiting for your arrival." Off looked at the creature and said, "Anyone for tennis ?" Immediately a tennis court appeared. Off was playing against a hermaphrodite composed of Pancho Gonzalez and Babe Didrickson. Off won each game handily, got back in his Ferrari and drove off. Suddenly, he was hurtling through a tunnel at breakneck speed. He saw a being of light resembling Ed Sullivan. Sullivan welcomed him to the really big show and Off was suddenly trading quips with Myron Cohen. The crowd laughed uproariously and begged for more. Off apologized but said he had to get back. The Beatles then appeared and sang "Get Back." With this, Off awoke with a start.

The dream had left him with a mixture of euphoria and dread. It had been great to be adored by these creatures. Yet, he had always had an irrational fear of being captured by Ed Sullivan and placed on his show to perform. He had felt this way ever since he had first seen this show as an immigrant in the early sixties. Dr. Anal had said that the phobia merely indicated a deep seated performance anxiety. The Sullivan show was a symbolic sexual arena, where Hans felt obligated to please the audience (his symbolic sexual partner). Although Off did not entirely discount this interpretation, it never seemed to help him. If he even saw any stiff older man folding his arms he would break out in a sweat. He avoided all Sullivanian (Harry Stack Sullivan-not Ed) training seminars. He even stopped watching Johnny Carson because his sidekick was named Ed. Now he was dreaming about Big Ed himself. It was just too much. His inner torment had reached the boiling point. He dialed Dr. Anal but reached Roto-Rooter instead. He redialed and got Dr. Anal's answering machine.

"Gut evening, thees is Dr. Otto B. Anal. I am a very busy, important analyst. You are probably a patient. So you must wait Ja. When I have ein break, I vill call you back, Ja. Why should I call you "back "when your name is Hilda or Wilhelm or Wolfgang or whatever. Just a little joke. Humor is gut, Ja. Freud told us dat. Just leave ein message at the beep, Ja ???"

Off hated that message. How could Otto be busy when he was so upset? However, past experience told him that he would soon calm down from his Sullivan-phobia. He remembered that by saying, "Ed is dead, Ed is dead, Ed is dead," and knew that he would mellow out soon enough.

Just as he was finishing his last "Ed is dead," his receptionist, Ms. Mizz walked in.

"Oh, I'm sorry Doctor. I didn't realize you were busy. I just wanted to tell you that your next patient was early, Mr. Whiplash? Snidely Off answered.

"No, Liebfraumilch."

"Liebfraumilch Whiplash?"

"That's what he says."

"This is just too intense, I have a patient named Liebfraumilch Whiplash?

Hastily he grabbed for the phone again and dialed Dr. Anal.

"Hallo, thees is Doktor Anal."

"Thank God...Otto, this is Hans. I'm freaking out. I'm hearing things, I'm seeing characters who are real people, I have a man named Liebfraumilch Whiplash in my waiting room."

"Have you been to the bathroom yet today Otto? You know a good bowel movement does wonders for the mind."

"Otto, are you listening to me? I am not constipated, I am losing my mind."

"Hansie, calm down and go to the toilette. It is amazing how relaxing dat could be, Ja. I vill see you for your regular appointment tomorrow, Ja."

"Ja, muttered Hans weakly. But how am I going to make it through today."

Despite the bizarre anal content of his conversation with Dr. Anal, he did feel a little better. He thought that maybe, just maybe he could face Mr. Whiplash, who was of course was suffering from neck pain, and post- traumatic stress disorder, due to an automobile accident. Things like that were always happening to Hans Off.

As far as Off knew Liebfraumilch was a type of wine, a German wine. He remembered his parents drinking it when he was young. Yet, he never remembered anyone who had this for a first name. His curiosity about the name was intense but he controlled himself and stuck to the content of the accident and its resultant symptoms. It seems that Mr. Whiplash was an insurance adjuster who took great delight in denying claims to save the company money. While out on the road adjusting a claim, he was struck in the rear by a truck carrying a load of bananas. The driver, a certain Mr. Mommalookabooboo, admitted he was drunk, though his blood showed no trace of alcohol. Mr. Mommalookabooboo explained that he was drunk with power, ever since he was elected president of the local Audobon Society.

Mr. Whiplash suffered contusions, confusions and E Pluribus Unums from the impact and was trying to collect. His company assigned their second best adjuster, Ms. Whiffenpoof to the case. Whiplash had long hated Whiffenpoof and she him. This was her chance to get even with Whiplash for singing the "whiffenpoof" song to her over a megaphone while she was adjusting her biggest claim. She was mortified, vilified and ossified and vowed to get even. Thus, she denied the claim, asserting that Mr. Mommalookabooboo was not really at fault, since there is no law against being drunk with power. Whiplash was so angry that his condition worsened and he had to be hospitalized.

Whiplash had heard that Off was an excellent hypnotist. Thus, upon being released from the hospital he had decided to give hypnosis a try.

"Hypnotize me doc!" said the angry adjuster.

"And what would we want to work on in the hypnotic state?" answered Off.

"I don't want this constant neck pain. Can't you just hypnotize me and tell it to go away ?"

"It doesn't work exactly like that, Mr. Whiplash. Your pain is a result of a physical trauma, complicated, by your anger at Mommalookabooboo and Whiffenpoof."

"What kind of mumbo jumbo is that? I just heard that hypnosis could relieve pain. Just tell me not to have pain and it will go away !"

"This is no mumbo jumbo. I think I can help you, but not with simple suggestion. You know Freud used simple suggestion and found that his results were short lived. That is one of the reasons he gave up on it. Hypnosis works much better when you make indirect suggestions for healing and a way that is compatible with the person's belief system. The person is encouraged to search his unconscious mind for a way of letting go of the chronic pain. It is important that the patient come up with the solution. He doesn't even have to know exactly how he has changed, as long as the inner change is made.

"Now, you really lost me, doc."

"Good, now that you are lost, you can wander around in your unconscious mind, until you are ready to go so deeply within that there is no need to understand what I am saying. When your unconscious is ready to review all sides of you neck problem, you'll find yourself getting more comfortable and your eyes will close."

Sure enough, Whiplashes' eyelids fluttered closed in a matter of seconds, a sure sign of hypnosis.

Off began: "Explore the many ways healing takes place. Which mode of healing is working for you? What are you doing now that your neck is completely healed? Now let your unconscious mind see how you are going to get from your present problem to a place where you are completely healed. Review some of the steps that you will be taking to ease your healing."

By this time, Whiplashes' entire demeanor had changed. His scowl was replaced by a relaxed yet wondering expression. As Off paused, Whiplashes' facial expression changed several times. At one point, he seemed to be re-living the traumatic accident. At another time he seemed angry. Finally after several minutes, he relaxed completely, falling into a deep reverie. Off noticed rapid eye movements. He had learned that this indicated and unconscious search for answers. When the rapid eye movements ceased, Off continued.

"When your unconscious mind knows it can continue the healing process on its own, and when your conscious mind can cooperate with the healing, you will start to stretch and yawn and open your eyes, returning to your usual state of consciousness. You will forget whatever you need to forget and remember whatever you need to remember."

Again, Off paused and waited. It took a few minutes, but Whiplash eventually began to stretch and yawn, just as he had been directed to.

"Wow ! Doc, I feel really spaced out, did you hypnotize me?"

"Yes, I did."

"How did you do that ? I mean I remember you told me to relax, and then my eyes were closed, and the next thing you know, I am awake. Wait a minute, my neck feels better. Wow, that's great."

Off was not used to such quick results. Usually, several sessions were required and the recovery was slow. Still, it was enjoyable to see such good results so quickly once in a while. Off, of course could never tell Anal that he was using Ericksonian hypnosis. Anal, as a strict Freudian, thought that these methods were inexcusable. After all, Whiplash had gained no insight and had not worked through all his anger. He just felt better. Dr. Off liked to help people feel better. It was cases like these that made him want to study psychology in the first place. He felt so good that he had temporarily forgotten about his voices and the historical characters that were parading through his life. Off smiled as Mr. Whiplash left, thanking him profusely for relieving his neck pain. However, his elevated mood was short lived. Ms. Mizz buzzed him to tell him his next appointment, Wyatt Earp was here.

Off flipped out. He lost it. His cookie of a mind crumbled, another ancient sheriff was coming for therapy. Why was this happening to him? Ms. Mizz ran in to see what the commotion was, only to be jumped and tied up by the now maniacal psychologist. After binding and gagging Ms. Mizz, Off ran out the door shouting, "Hee Haw. I'm headed for Dodge City boys. I'm gonna git me some cowgirl and paint the town red. He Haw."

CHAPTER 8

The Chase

Off was off and running. His gait out of the office resembled the canter of a thoroughbred race horse. As he careened into the crowded street he was almost hit by a taxi. The driver called him a "f----n lunatic".

"Thank you very much" said Off, "I am returning to the moon soon."

Racing down 99th street, he hung a right on Broadway and made it as far as Zabars' Delicatessen. By this time, he was being chased by two police officers. At Zabars', Off crashed into a wall. It was not a physical wall. It was an olfactory wall. It was a wall created by the splendiferous odors of the deli. He smelled lox and bagels, whitefish and sable, creamed herring and most of all apple strudel. The melange of odors stopped Off dead in his tracks in front of Zabar's.

"Ooh, ooh, he's stopping at Zabars," said the first policeman, "let's get him." Off couldn't remember who he was or why he was running, but he ducked into Zabars' just ahead of the huffing and puffing policemen. The aisles were crowded with shoppers, pushing each other as only New Yorkers could. The sight of a police chase inside the store provoked a mixture of reactions. Some shoppers bolted out of the way. Others shouted obscenities. One elderly gentleman tried to grab Off, shouting "citizen's arrest, citizen's arrest." It was as if the keystone cops were chasing the road runner during rush hour at Grand Central Station. Off might have escaped if he had not dove into the barrel of half sour pickles. To say he was "in a pickle" was to say the least. It was here amidst the briny cucumbers that the police officers handcuffed the beleaguered psychologist and read him his rights. "You have the right to remain silent. You have the right to be represented by an attorney..." Stop !!" yelled Off, "I want my attorney. The police escorted the now meek headshrinker to police headquarters and let him call his lawyer. Off quickly dialed the number and the receptionist answered, "Dewey, Cheatham and Howe." Still in a trancelike stupor, Off asked to speak to Mr. Howe. Off was beginning to accept the reality of his world of T V characters. He knew Mr. Howe as the top litigator in the firm. He was born in Louisiana, on the Bayou. It was later known as "Howe's Bayou."

"Mr. Howe isn't in. would you like to speak to Mr. Shyster?"

"Is he the only one there?"

"I'm afraid so," answered the receptionist.

"Okay, this is an emergency, put him on."

"Mr. Shyster here."

"Yes,....this is Dr. Hans Off..."

"Hey wait a minute buddy, my hands have been off since I got married."

"No, my name is Dr. Hans Off and I've been arrested, and I need a lawyer..."

"All right doctor, where are you ?"

"I'm not sure, Officers Goody and Twoshoes arrested me and..."

"Goody and Twoshoes, huh...?"

"Doctor, I suggest you get a doctor, before they take you to Blueview ?"

"That's where they said they were taking me."

"Well, have a good trip, see you next Fall"

Off grimaced at the old joke. He needed help and this buffoon was throwing ancient" one liners" at him. He might as well have called Benny Oldman. At this point, a police officer, whose real names were not Goody or Twoshoes, arrived. Officer Dumkopf walked in, riding his horse, Schmartkopf. "Look, Officer Dumkopf. . ."

"Call me Dummy."

"O.K., Dummy, listen I'm a real person, somehow I got lost in this world which seems to have half real people, and half historical characters from the nineteenth and twentieth centuries.

"And who did you see now, Wyatt Earp?"

"Yes."

"Doc, I think you need to read some Sartre. "Wait a minute, I think I have the classic comic of "Being and Nothingness" right here..."

"That's what Rumplestilskin said..."

"You mean the Rumplestilskin?"

"Yeah."

"I know Rump, he and I went to school together."

"I know, the school For Scary studies in Erie Pennsylvania."

"That's right, brilliant fellow, great straw spinner too...anyway, this Sartre was able to distinguish between Being and Nothingness. He stated that we are ultimately created by our decisions. Each man must therefore bravely make decisions, and take responsibility for his decisions even in the absence of any eternal meaning in the universe. In short, we create ourselves out of the bleak nothingness of being. It is the same for historic characters or live human beings. We create ourselves. Therefore, your problem is not a problem. It doesn't matter if I am real or not. We are all equally real and unreal. You can just relax and get back to your practice of 'shrinkology' on West End Avenue."

Off was stunned. If this man were right, his entire cosmology, theology and psychology would be turned upside down. Man would no longer be created in God's image. He would be his own creation. The same would be true of historic characters. Once they were alive, they were always alive...in a way. In fact, due to the magic of film, video tape, dvds and Netflix downloads, they might last on Earth longer than (so called) contemporary, real people. Off was feeling a little better until he was interrupted by several men in white coats who began strapping him into a strait jacket.

"Let's go buddy," said the tall one.

"But where are we going ?"

In a peculiar singsong voice, the short one began to say, "We're going to take you away, ha ha, ho, ho, hee, hee, to the funny farm, where life is happy and gay, hee-hee and life is beautiful all the time..." Off let out a loud piercing scream which actually broke a glass in the hand of the clerk. (who looked remarkably like Ella Fitzgerald).

"Who are you anyway ?" Off said to the short man in the white coat.

"Napoleon the twenty second" he replied, as he subdued Off and placed him on a gurney.

"Let's go."

CHAPTER 9

The Funny Farm

Off must have passed out for a while. He came to his senses just as the ambulance turned off First Avenue, into the emergency room. He caught a glimpse of the sign, **Blueview**. Hans knew that this meant trouble. He wasn't going to some nice expensive rest home, where neurotic housewives went for stress reduction. He was going to a place where the New York City cops sent the patients they could not deal with. He might be evaluated by a doctor that went to school in Upper Volta. And Upper Volta didn't even exist anymore.

Of course, considering recent events, Off should have realized he would be evaluated not by someone from Upper Volta, but a doctor from the distant past. It was not a great surprise then when the E.R. doctor popped his head in and said, "Hi, I'm Doctor Louis Pasteur." Dr. Pasteur said he was doing a psychiatric residency in the Blueview of Hans Off's mind. Dr. Pasteur was well known for inventing the process for purifying milk. But what was a nineteenth-century doctor doing in a twenty-first century emergency room? Off was clearly upset at being in the emergency room. If he was flipping out, he wanted to be at a nice place, with rooms designed by interior decorators. Yet, here he was in a big hospital, being examined by a famous nineteenth-century doctor. Pasteur didn't care much for psychiatric emergencies. He preferred blood and gore to fear and trembling. At least you could stop bleeding, but anxiety was another thing. Thorazine aside, what could you do about a

186

vague sense of dread? How could you cure the sickness of the soul that these psychiatric patients came in with? With these rosy thoughts on his mind, Pasteur popped his head into Off's cubicle in the E.R.

When Off saw that he was dealing with another historic character, he became enraged. " I want a real doctor," he shouted. "I want my mentor, I want Otto B. Anal." This was all very amusing to Pasteur.

"What a name, 'Otto B. Anal. "Did your doctor have a rough time with his toilet training?"

"As a matter of fact he did." replied Off, gruffly. "But that doesn't matter, I want to see him, not you."

Pasteur shrugged his shoulders and wrote an order for thorazine, 500 milligrams, stat.

Pasteur didn't feel good about writing that order. But what else could he do? The guy was delusional, thought that Pasteur was a nineteenth-century doctor. Off began to get violent and insisted he had an <u>analyst</u> named Anal. What can you do with a guy like that. So he pumped him with thorazine and sent him off to the psych ward for observation.

Off slept for 48 hours. He slept so deeply and for so long that even the nurses were getting upset. The nurses knew from experience that if you gave thorazine to a patient who was <u>not</u> psychotic, you would produce a condition of prolonged sleep, almost resembling stupor. That is exactly what happened to Off.

He was awakened by a man screaming in his ear, "The Giants win the pennant, the Giants win the pennant, I don't believe it, I don't believe it, I will not believe it." Drowsily, Off looked at the man and asked who he was.

"Why I'm Russ Hodges and we're here at the Polo Grounds at the most exciting moment in baseball history."

As the cobwebs started to clear from his brain, Off realized that this man thought it was 1951. He was calling Bobby Thompson's homer, "the shot heard round the world." In fact, Off remembered hearing about it in his part of the world, Vienna. One enterprising merchant renamed his Bratwurst, "Thompsonwurst," and his sauerkraut, "Brancakraut." But even the thorazine couldn't make Off forget who he was and what the year was. Off thought, "I'm Dubledoctor Hans Off, its 2015 and this guy is a nut." "Imagine a paranoid schizophrenic who thinks he's Russ Hodges. He could at least have thought he was Gil Hodges." Gradually Off remembered that he was in Blueview. Although he had been doubting his own sanity, he did not feel he belonged in a place where people thought they were old baseball announcers. Tim McCarver he could have handled, but Russ Hodges?

CHAPTER 10

Anal's Analysis

Off was so insistent about seeing his analyst, that a nurse finally looked the name up on her i-phone, just to shut him up. To her surprise, the Google search revealed an Otto B. Anal. When she called, he was in his office. So she left a message that one of his patients was at Blueview. When Otto got the message, he could feel his anal sphincter tightening. "That nincompoop Off, what kind of mess is he in now?" Anal asked the nurse. After carefully calculating the location of clean toilets between his office and Blueview, Anal hopped into a cab that whisked him downtown.

When Anal Arrived, Off was deep in a discussion with the alleged Russ Hodges. They were arguing about who was on deck when Thompson hit the homer. Off was sure it was Willie Mays. Hodges insisted it was Don Meuller. Anal ignored the debate and shouted, "Vas ist Los Hans ?"

"Der hund ist Los." Off answered, instinctively.

"Otto...am I glad to see you," he stammered, "get me outta here."

"Eine minute," averred Otto, "Eine kleine minute."

"First tell me what you are doing in this place."

Hans was scared. He didn't really want to admit to his esteemed mentor what was really happening to him, so he decided to lie through his teeth.

"I was framed, Otto. A deranged patient said I was Raskolnikov. She said I was threatening to kill a certain Ima Badanov. The next thing I know, the police are picking me up and taking me here."

"Hans"

"Yes, Otto."

"You are lying."

"I know I am Otto."

"Then, tell me the truth!!!" He thundered.

"Follow along with me panel, as I read this affadavit, I..."

"Hans, I just want you to tell me the truth!"

"Oh, but...Otto, you won't believe me."

"Try me."

At that, Off collapsed in a veil of tears and told the entire story, the voices, the characters, the chase and the arrest.

Otto just listened, rubbed his goatee and said, "I see...I see...I see."

Hans hated when Otto listened and said "I see." It seemed to indicate that he had a theory but did not want to say it yet. Otto always preferred to get the patient to develop his own theory. Only as a last resort would he actually make what was called a complete "genetic interpretation." This misleading term had nothing to do with genes, DNA or the like. It meant that both the immediate and original causes of the maladaptive behavior had been accounted for. This would then free the patient to act in his or her own best interest, without being burdened by the original trauma.

Otto B. Anal was beginning to formulate a theory, but he did not want to make any premature interpretations so he just muttered, "I see, I see." Anal suspected that Off's trouble started during the anal stage (3-5 years old) and had something to do with his toilet training. Anal had always thought that Off's utter lack of concern for toilet theory and bathroom time had serious psychological consequences. Off practically disregarded the anal stage in helping his own patients and spent almost no time on the pot. When questioned about this by Anal, he merely stated that his excrement came out immediately upon sitting down. So why should he spend any time sitting there ?

"Don't you want to make sure it's all out?" the astounded Anal would comment. "I could always come back," answered Off. All this was very weird to Otto B. Anal. The fact that Off was in the midst of some sort of breakdown strengthened his conviction that something had gone wrong with Off's toilet training.

As Anal continued to mutter "I see..." Off began to get angry. "Otto, I know you have a theory, and I want to hear it."

"You're not going to like it, Hans."

"Oy vey", not that toilet training stuff again."

"Off, why are you such a nut-job? Toilet training is important, toilet training is very important."

Off felt something snap in his mind when his beloved mentor insisted on the anal interpretation of his troubles. All he could say was "horse-feathers," before he sunk into a deep trance. Suddenly, Dr. Anal looked like a cartoon character. He had a big cigar and a square moustache. Off blinked, in disbelief. That is until the character said, "So tell me Otto, how long have you been hearing these voices?" In a robotic monotone, Off answered, "About three weeks Otto, I mean...I don't know what I mean..."

"That's the most ridiculous thing I ever heard." said Anal, unconsciously.

It was at this point that Off disappeared. That is- he thought he disappeared. He no longer felt he had a body. Yet, somehow, there was some sort of awareness or consciousness of self. Off felt he was floating, high up in the corner of the room. As he looked down, he could see himself, Hans Off talking to Otto B. Anal. Amazingly, he could even hear the conversation.

He saw his body freeze as Dr. Anal began to shout, "Toilet training, toilet training." He wanted to answer. He wanted to cry hysterically at not being heard or understood by this caricature of an analyst. But he couldn't move. He didn't understand what was happening to him. Maybe I'm dead, he thought. But if he were dead, why did he still feel alive and aware. He continued to watch as Anal called to an attendant:

"This man is seriously ill, he's catatonic, get me some liquid thorazine, stat!" Off watched Anal inject the thorazine into his arm when, all of a sudden, everything went black. Through the magic of chemistry, Hans Off was back in his body, but boy did he feel like s--t.

Off awoke and once again tried to remember where he was. His body felt like he had just gone fifteen rounds with a young boxer. "But at least

I still have a body," he thought. By utilizing all his willpower, he was able to press the buzzer for a nurse. Half an hour later, woman resembling an old fashioned nurse, pointed hat and all came into the room.

"Ah, Dr. Off are you feeling better now?"

"I just want to get out of here."

"We'll just have to see, won't we."

Off decided not to mention that she looked like a nineteenth-century nurse. He was beginning to realize that you can only trust certain people with the truth. Although he didn't yet know what was happening to him or why, he did know that most people, especially his Freudian psychoanalyst did not understand. This momentous decision coincided with the return of another inner voice. It was Dr. Moley's turn.

CHAPTER 11

· ·

The Cosmic Chuckle

"Psst, Off." There it was again.

"Who is it ?"

"It's me, Dr. Ho Lee Moley, I am another one of your spiritual guides, like Dr. Groddek"

"Oh boy Ho Lee, I'm in big trouble, I'm locked up in Bluevue, neutralized with thorazine and now I'm hearing another spirit guide. How do I know you aren't a schizophrenic voice?"

"I tell you only good and useful things, that is what a spirit guide does, I can help you if you will let me."

"Yeah, how?"

"By teaching you about the great cosmic chuckle."

"All right, I'll bite, what is a cosmic chuckle, some sort of large, gooey candy, sprinkled with sugar."

"No, Hans, those are chuckles candies. These are giggles, ha has, laughs."

"Boy, could I use a laugh."

"Hans, you have to see that it's all very funny. Take for example your name, Hans Off."

"So, big deal."

"Well, some people might think that a former chiropractor named Hans Off is funny."

"Oh"

"Then take for example your doctor, Otto B. Anal, the toilet man."

"Yeah, I can see what you mean. But how can being locked up in a psych ward be funny?"

"Have you met Benny Oldman or Goody Threeshoes yet ?"

"No."

"Hoo boy, just wait. You see Otto we never really know why things happen, what they will lead to, or what anything means. Things that seem terrible often lead to great knowledge and growth."

"Again, the New Age crap."

"Otto, just listen, were you happy with your life before we started talking to you?"

"No-o- but..."

"Then why not be open-minded and try to learn something from the whacko adventures you're having?"

"But the whacko adventures are my life..."

"Exactly, when you look at things differently, they can be very amusing. If you listen very carefully, you can hear God chuckling at this giant sitcom you call your life. When you begin to chuckle with Him/Her (God), the impact is cosmic. It's like getting a rush of Nirvana in the Garden of Eden. Next time you are tempted to get angry at your 'fate', try saying, "Thanks for everything, I have no complaint whatsoever. Then begin to chortle, guffaw, giggle and roar with delight.'"

"That's nuts"

"Exactly, it's so nuts that it works, then you can begin to grasp the true meaning of all that is."

"I don't know"

"That's right, you don't know much, so why not try the cosmic chuckle, what have you got to lose?"

"All right, all right, maybe you have a point. I'll give it a try."

Off wasn't sure, but despite the overdose of thorazine, he did feel a little bit better.

"Thanks for everything." he muttered, "I have no complaint whatsoever."

CHAPTER 12

Benny Oldman

Benny Oldman had been hospitalized in Blueview since 1952. At that time he was listed as a paranoid schizophrenic with delusions of grandeur. His delusion was the idea that he was a comedian. He had a compulsion to tell jokes, mostly quick one- liners. "Take my strife, please." was his favorite. This was a bit strange, since he wasn't married and had no strife. But that didn't stop Benny. He just pumped out the one-liners until his family hospitalized him out of desperation. And there he sat, telling jokes, in a hospital, where his humor was met by everything from silly laughter to icy stares.

As Off opened his eyes from the IV thorazine, the first thing he saw was Benny. "A guy walked into a doctor's office..."

"Say what..." muttered Off sleepily.

"A guy walked into a doctor's office, the doctor gives him six months to live...the guy doesn't pay his bill...the doctor gives him another six months." Ba dum dum (a drum roll).

Off chuckled at the old joke.

"A guy walks into a psychiatrist's office...says good morning...
The psychiatrist says, "I wonder what he means by that?" Ba dum dum.
This time Off laughed out loud.

"Who are you?"

"I'm Benny Oldman, master comedian, king of the one- liners."

"But, what are you doing here?"

"Oh, my family thinks I'm nuts. So do the doctors."

"And what is allegedly wrong with you?"

"Well, for one thing, I tell jokes all the time. They say I'm inappropriate. For another thing they don't like my jokes. And finally, there's my philosophy."

"You are locked up because you have a philosophy ?"

"Oh yes, It's a philosophy they feel is dangerous."

"O.K., what is it ?"

"Fun."

"Fun is dangerous ?"

"Absolutely."

"I believe people should have fun all the time. They should enjoy their work. They should get pleasure from their kids. They should even have fun doing the laundry. You see, I believe life should be pleasurable, gratifying and meaningful."

"So, why is this allegedly dangerous?"

"Because the sewers would get backed up."

"Sewers?"

"That's right, who would work for roto-rooter if life was supposed to be fun. Who would be an accountant? Who would sell life insurance?"

"I see what you mean."

"No you don't. You see, there are actually people who like to unclog sewers, crunch numbers and sell insurance.

"Really?"

"Yes, really."

"And how did this philosophy come to you?"

"Well, in 1952, I had a dream. It was a vivid dream, unlike any other I have ever had. I went into an altered state of consciousness and the voice of God spoke to me. It said, "Benny, make people laugh." So I answered, "But nobody likes my jokes."

So God says, "So get a captive audience." The next thing I see, is a vision of myself telling jokes in a hospital ward. These people are mostly out of their mind, but they know one thing that the people on the outside don't know."

"What's that?"

"They know that, in actuality, the Earth is a remedial planet."

A "remedial planet?"

"That's right, a place where the developmentally challenged are sent to learn the basic lessons about life and death."

"Let me get this straight, you think that the purpose of the Earth is to provide a place for developmentally challenged souls to learn lessons?"

"Exactly, you see, most people on Earth are basically selfish. They want, whatever they want and they want it now, like healthy two-year olds! If they get what they think they want, they want more of it. If they have extra, they store it away in case they run out."

"So, what's wrong with that ?"

"Well, first off, they have a warped idea of what they want."

They think they want "stuff". So they spend all their time trying to get "stuff". The ones who don't get much "stuff" moan and groan that it's unfair. This creates the hell of righteous indignation. They are angry and feel they have a right to be angry. They just go round and round with this ire until they die of bitterness. The ones that have a lot of "stuff" are afraid of the first group. They are afraid they will lose their "stuff" so they buy insurance and dead bolt locks. Their constant fear of losing their stuff consumes them until they die of stress and fear."

"That's some ugly picture you are painting."

"Ugly, yes, but true on this remedial planet."

"I suppose, you know what to do to remedy this nasty situation?"

"Of course, I already told you. Have fun. Get loose. If you're poor, have fun. If you're rich, have fun. Do work that you like. Laugh with your friends, live in whatever style of life feels right to you and be grateful for it all."

"That sounds like what Dr. Ho Lee Mo Lee just told me."

"You know Ho Lee ?"

"Well, sort of, he's actually a disembodied voice I hear."

"Far out, me too, he really is a hoot, isn't he?"

"Actually, now that you mention it, he does make some sense, but it's so impractical."

"Practical, shmactical. All I know is that ever since I started listening to that impractical stuff, I've been very happy."

"Give me a break. You are on the locked ward of a hospital. You are in prison."

"You may think that, but I feel as free as a bird. I am following my path, which is to tell jokes to psychiatric patients until they realize that they don't have to suffer anymore. The only point of suffering, you know, is to learn how to stop suffering."

"I think you are really whacko. The next thing you'll be telling me is that 'love' is the answer to all problems."

"Correct. If people learned to laugh together, they could tolerate each other. If they could tolerate each other, they could even learn to love each other (or at least heavy like).

"But these are such cliches. In real life, nobody gives a crap about anyone else, let alone anyone a little different from them. "That's where the "laughatron" comes in."

"Laughatron?"

"Yes, It's a device that sends out invisible sonic waves that sound like laughing. These waves activate the hypothalamus gland to produce endorphins and other pleasurable brain chemicals. Soon, the people start to laugh. It feels so good, that others around them begin to chortle. Lutherans laugh with Jews. Episcopalians laugh with Catholics. Buddhists laugh with Zoroastrians. And here's where the beauty comes in. They are having such fun, that they forget to hate the others who are a little different. They begin to realize that we are all just regulation humans, on a remedial planet who are regaining the capacity to have fun and be whoever they are."

"You mean they forget, hate, greed and envy ?"

"They forget all that garbage and just "get down.'"

"So where is this laughatron?"

"If I told you, you wouldn't find it."

"You mean I have to find it myself?"

"Yup."

And with that, Benny ran off to tell some "one liners" to some mental patients who had heard all his jokes before.

Off observed their reactions carefully for any sign of laughter, joy or remission of psychotic symptoms. All he saw though, was a lot of blank stares and shuffling feet. Things were happening too fast. Was this philosophy viable or was it a mixture of old religion and new- age nonsense ? For some unexplainable reason, at that particular moment, it seemed profound beyond Off's wildest dreams.

Despite the hope inspired by the philosophy of laughter, Off yearned for the simple life he once knew; patients with severe issues, orthodox Otto B Anal and delicious trysts with Lola Palooza. Speaking of Lola, where was she anyway? In the" hubbub" of hospitalization, he needed the comfort, love and sexuality of the woman he loved.

CHAPTER 13

Lola Returns

At three o'clock, on the third day of his hospitalization, Lola bounced into Hans' hospital ward. Hans was so glad to see her, he barely noticed that she smelled like a broom closet.

"Why do you smell like a broom closet?" he inquired.

"Why are you asking such a silly question?"

"I don't know, the only other person who ever smelled like that was the doctor who examined me in the waiting room, Dr. Whiskers or something."

"That's Dr. Twistoff..."

"Right, how did you know?"

"Never mind, let's take a look at you Hans. Are you feeling any better?"

"Actually, I never, felt that bad. It's just that I was getting confused, hearing voices, seeing fictional characters."

"Hansie, you are very sick, but don't worry, you'll get better."

"But Lola, I am not sick, just confused."

"That's what they all say."

"I know, but this is different. I don't think I'm having a nervous breakdown."

"And what would you call disembodied voices, fictional characters in your office and jabbering conversations with mental patients?"

"I'm not sure what it is yet, I only know it's not what it seems."

"Hans, get a grip. Let Otto analyze you so we can return to our happy life together."

"I would like nothing more, but I think Otto is too anal. Maybe, I need a new shrink."

This disappointed Lola, as she kind of liked Otto. She thought he was cute, in an anal retentive way. But she had to respect Hans and his wishes.

"Hans, you seem nuttier than a fruitcake to me, but you should have a doctor who you can relate to, let me see if I can find someone a little more advanced. I just want my old Hans back."

"Good, you'll get a better model Hans back. Just get me another doctor!"

CHAPTER 14

Xavier Istential Ph.D.

Lola had had it with orthodox medical doctors. She always liked psychologists better anyway. But how would she find the right doctor for Hans? She thought of the New York State Psychological Association. But they were too straight to listen to this story. She thought of asking her yoga teacher but he was all tied up. Finally, she did the logical thing and googled "shrinks with doctorates." Looking under this title there was a bewildering array of names, web sites and satisfaction ratings. Most of the web sites promised a complete cure for everything from stress and anxiety to plantar warts. The names were even more confusing, Dr. Lipschitz, Dr. Asstalks, Dr. Heine, Dr. Fanny, Dick Hertz, Ph.D. ("Who's Dick Hertz?" she asked herself).

After several minutes of pondering, her eye caught a small web site which seemed intriguing, "Xavier Istential, Ph.D. Genetic Epistemology, Psychotherapy, Electric Pretzel Therapy." Now, Lola was pretty bright, but she had no idea what Genetic Epistemology was, or for that matter, electric-pretzel therapy. She did know psychotherapy, however, and this interesting web page attested to this man's competence in that area. Thus, Lola let her fingers do the texting and held her breath, waiting to see what kind of response she would get. Lola had a theory that the first contact with a person would tell you how the rest of the relationship would go. As she texted, her anticipation became more acute. Her heart began to pound and her breathing got shallow. Finally, a response, "Dr.

X. Istential, I cure your crises and vices, How may I help you?" Lola was a little taken aback by the informal greeting, and texted back "Homina, homina...well, er, I think..."

"My boyfriend needs a new therapist," she wrote "he has a therapist, Otto B. Anal, but Otto is too anal, so..." "chortle...chortle "was the response from Dr. X Istential. "Continue, please, I'm sorry, sometimes names can be funny."

Lola texted a very abbreviated version of Hans' story and was very impressed by the responses the new doctor made. He said it sounded like an existential identity crisis and that that was his specialty. He promised to visit the very next day and Lola felt very relieved.

X. Istential was intrigued by this new case. He glanced at his note pad and saw that he had written a few notes during the telephone conversation, "Voices, characters, positive messages, laughter, laughatron." "What the heck is a laughatron? he wondered. Little did he know the role the role the laughatron was to play in the rest of his life.

CHAPTER 15

....

The Holy Laughatron

X. Istential arrived at Bluevue a few minutes early for his first interview with Hans Off. He thought of the old joke, "If a patient is late, he is passive-aggressive. If he is early, he is anxious. If he is on time, he's obsessive-compulsive." He chuckled to himself at the joke and made a mental note to use it as soon as he could. When he introduced himself at the nurse's station, he was struck by the thought that this case would somehow be important. "Just an odd hunch," he thought, though he did not notice that he was hunched over like Igor in Young Frankenstein ("that's I gore...").

At the moment he laid his eyes on Hans Off, he knew that his hunch was correct. "Frog," he said.

"Frog?" answered Off.

"Yes, Frog Off" Suddenly, Off remembered. As a small boy in Vienna, he had a curious penchant for leaping onto lily pads. Once, he almost drowned and was rescued by an older boy named.....What was his name. It was something odd....Yorick...No..No..No..Zeigezunt....No... Xavier !!!! That was it, Xavier!!!!

"Allow me to introduce myself, Xavier Istential, Ph.D. At your service once again, Frog Off." A torrent of thoughts and images related to childhood flooded through Off's' beleaguered mind. Yes, it was him. It was a grown up version of the boy who saved his life in childhood. What a wacky coincidence. But things like that were always happening to

Hans Off. Jung would have called this synchronicity. Off had a need to be saved again, albeit psychologically this time. It was somehow connected to the appearance of the one person who had saved him, physically such a long time ago.

"At least he's not a weird fantasy character," thought Off.

"It's so good to see you again Hans. Tell me, do you still think you are a frog?" This was a careful jest. It was specifically designed to see if Off could laugh. If he could laugh, he couldn't be too depressed. Off chortled, "No, but I do hear voices and see old historic characters as real people."

"And who have you seen ?"

Off breathed a sigh of relief at the serious inquiry. This man really seemed to want to know the world of Hans Off. Without pre-judgment, he could try to see things the way this patient saw them. Then, and only then, he could offer a therapeutic opinion.

"I have seen Wyatt Earp, Dr. Louis Pasteur, Russ Hodges. I even saw Rumplestilskin!" Go on.."

Dr. Anal thinks I'm nuts, that my whole problem is related to toilet training."

"How so?"

This was great. This guy was asking Off to think, something Otto had never mentioned.

"I don't know exactly. Something about repressed rage at being forced to control myself and use a toilet."

"No s--t?"

"Clever, anyway supposedly I am taking the rage and using it to create a fantasy world, a sort of displacement and sublimation. This enables civilization to function and me to continue to hear voices and interact with the fantasy characters I love."

"And what do you think of this interpretation?"

"It's shit, chicken s--t, bull s--t, elephant s--t."

"That's what my mentor, Fritz Perls used to say!"

"I get the point."

"I want to figure this thing out. I know it has significance. But I think my Freudian friend has reached his limit."

205

X Istential was careful not to criticize Otto. He felt that the Freudians had some good points. After all, Freud was responsible for pioneering the importance of the unconscious, interpreting dreams, pointing out the importance of resistance and transference. Yet, Freudians tended to get bogged down in theory and technique. They tended to say too little and to interpret everything in terms of sex and aggression. Anxiety and depression were always rooted in the past. As an existentialist, X. felt that anxiety was created more by how people dealt with the impending future. For all real danger lurked in the future, especially death. The other key issues, responsibility, freedom and meaning, always seemed to complete the equation for people who were having trouble dealing with their life.

Hans Off was certainly having trouble dealing with his life. Though he seemed to have it made, he was constantly fending off anxiety and depression. Not only that, even though he was sixty-seven, he had never married. Not even the alluring Ms. Lola Palooza could pin him down. Thus, as he listened to Off tell his story, he began to formulate theories as to what was causing these strange happenings. Did he have trouble limiting his freedom and taking responsibility for his decisions? Is that why he didn't marry Lola? Did he find his life increasingly meaningless as he relentlessly marched into middle age? Did he feel alone and isolated in the hostile world? Finally, was his fear of death (which he had always had) increasing with age? These hypotheses would all be tested as reasons for the development of voices, characters and the like. For now, he had to develop a rapport with Dr. Off by inquiring about his current reality and the past which led him to be this way.

X. always liked the direct approach in beginning a case.

Thus, after Offs' tirade about Dr. Anal, X. got right down to business.

"So, Hans, how come you're such a loony- toon ?"

The blunt question took Off aback at first. Then he laughed.

"It does sound absurd doesn't it? I mean, how could historical characters be parading through my life as if they were live people? And why am I hearing voices telling me that I have some sort of psycho-spiritual mission or quest. I sound like someone out of a Blues Brothers movie."

X. got serious for a moment and replied, "Hans, it is very difficult to separate fantasy from reality. In our culture, we call people who hear voices and see things that aren't there, paranoid schizophrenics. There are some exceptions though, for example, in the Bible, didn't Abraham hear the voice of God telling him to bind and kill his son Isaac? Didn't Moses hear the voice of God tell him to go free the Jewish slaves ? Were these Biblical heroes paranoid schizophrenics ?

Off was stunned. This guy was making sense. Maybe there was a difference between the voices heard by madmen and the voices heard by spiritual heroes. But then again, Off did not yet place himself in a class with Abraham or Moses. It was just that he didn't feel crazy. He was just puzzled by his perceptions which were clearly beyond the usual range of human experience. What he liked about his new doctor was the open inquiring attitude. He was not quick to reduce these phenomena to any particular cause.

Though Off suspected his new doctor might have theories about his affliction (as, of course he did), he did not let the theories interfere with an exploration of the meaning of the experiences for the patient. Off didn't know just how to answer the direct question. If Otto had asked that question, he would have been afraid to answer. With this guy, he just knew that the question was a jesting way of probing his true feelings about himself.

"Do you think I'm a loony tune?" inquired Off.

"Actually, no. The reason I asked it that way is that I think you think that about yourself."

"I guess you're right doctor..."

"Please, call me X."

"Well X., I guess I am a little disturbed by my predicament. I mean, a few months ago, I was sailing along, with a successful practice, a great girlfriend, a boundless future..."

"You felt the future was boundless?"

"Yes, of course..."

"What about death?"

"But I'm young and healthy."

"So you were acting like you are immortal ?"

"I guess so, well, maybe I am. You know a lot of philosophies say you don't really die..."

"That may or may not be true, but it rarely seems to stop any of us from having anxiety about death. Even those firmly convinced about reincarnation seem to retain death anxiety."

"But what about all those people that say they don't fear death?"

"They are one of two things, advanced spiritual masters or death deniers."

"Which one do you think I am?"

"Are you an advanced spiritual master?"

"No."

"There you have it."

"There I have what."

"There you have the beginning of where to look for the cause of your woes."

"Hmmmmm."

CHAPTER 16

The Denial of Death

"So you really think I am denying death, doctor.?"

"Please call me X.""

"O.K., why do you think that?"

"Well, a man by the name of Becker, Ernest, not Arnie, wrote a book by that name. Dr. Becker was a brilliant anthropologist. His theory was that we are a death denying culture because death is so terrifying. Dr. Becker felt that the only way we could go on living was by pretending that we would never die."

"But X, I admit I am terrified of death. So how can I be a death denier?"

"You see Hans, even though you admit you are afraid of death, you seek reassurance that somehow you will be spared-after all you were a healer of bodies, as a chiropractor and now you are a healer of souls as a psychologist."

"So what....I am still going to die!"

"Yes, your body will die but maybe something of you could go on."

"Yes, I have explored those theories. I believe in reincarnation, karma, and the eternal soul!"

"So, then, why are you so afraid of death?"

"I guess you are right! Maybe if I review my entire current situation, my fears will diminish."

"Now we are getting somewhere. What then could all these historical characters be doing in your life?"

"What if they are like spirit guides, trying to expunge my fear of death and lead me to the truth of my great cosmic lesson plan!"

"Bingo, Hans. Your insight is off the charts. You are so smart. Now you just have to listen to these guides, follow your heart and your gut intuition, and surrender to the higher power."

"Yeah, but what is the nature of this higher power?"

"Well, I don't want to pretend to have all the answers, but I think it is the great source of all being…that is why they called old time magicians sorcerers!"

"Ohhh…wow, yeah, far out, …..sorcerers… So I have to reunite with my source?"

"Yes, exactly right. I recommend meditation and prayer. Pray as if there is no action needed. Then take action like there is no such thing as prayer!"

"Wow, far out again, yeah."

"You see Hans, many New Age gurus tell you they have the Secret. You can get whatever you want, just think positive, affirm the positive and you'll get the 'stuff' you want. This is partially true. You can get better stuff and even adulation from the world as a success but still be unhappy." "Ugh, then what is the real answer? Well, after you pray, you have to meditate. You can just concentrate on a mantra, like "Om" for 20 minutes, twice a day. This results in peace, better health and a lessening of anxiety. The reason is that you are connecting and becoming one with the source. This is called concentrative meditation."

He continued: "Or you can just sit down, watch you breathing and see your thoughts and feelings come up. You don't judge them or push them away, just observe. Eventually the truth comes to you. This is called awareness or insight meditation. Then you come back to the world and be a "mench."

"What is a mench?"

"It is a Yiddish word for a really good person, who loves himself and other people. He is not afraid of death, because he knows his soul is eternal. He does his thing in the world until he gets the meaning and point of his existence. Then he peacefully lives until it is time to drop the body and move on to a purely spiritual existence of some kind."

"Do we have awareness in the spiritual state?"

"Well, some theorists think we have a point of focus. Others think we just merge with the one source of being. Actually, it doesn't really matter now. Once you are meditating on the truth, the truth will come and set you free. You just surrender!"

"Wow, I need to process that, it is heavy duty that's for sure!"

X was really proud of his new patient. He was getting it better and faster than most patients.

CHAPTER 17

Hans Takes Off

Hans' head was spinning with his new insight. But his problems would have to wait. As soon as he got out of Blueview, he had to get back to his office to see a patient. Dr. Istential got him released quite quickly. Hans rushed back to his office to see his own patients.

His first case was unusual. Two legal secretaries, who worked together wanted his advice. As he walked into the office, Ms. Mizz whispered to him that there was a small problem. It seemed that the two girls were broke. Their boss, an attorney named Billy Eagle, was sick. He was an ill Eagle. The office, where they worked as paralegals, paid them minimum wage, without health insurance. Mr. Eagle, whose hobby was figure skating, was cheap. He was a cheap skate. They tried to get insurance with Obamacare but they couldn't get through to the website. They wanted to pay Dr. Off's fee in pretzels. "What do you think Hans?" said Ms. Mizz. "Well, what kind of pretzels?" answered Hans, cleverly. "You better ask them," replied Ms. Mizz. So Hans ushered Mary and Flo into the office.

"Nice pretzels" said Hans, trying not to stare at Mary's cleavage. "Are those the pretzels for payment?"

"No" responded Mary emphatically, "Flo and I bake pretzels. We can pay you with onion, sesame or low salt."

"Well, Okay, said Hans, "I'll take onion."

The girls seemed a little surprised that the doctor would accept pretzels for payment. Hans noticed their shock and said, "You see, what I do is not really about the money."

"It's not?" responded Mary. Then what do you get out of it?"

"Don't get me wrong," said Dr. Off. "Most of my patients have insurance or pay me directly. There is nothing wrong with that. But if someone cannot afford me and pays something of value to them, that is OK too. What I do is really about helping people. Essentially all of us are in the same boat. We are searching for meaning in our lives and need to discover out great cosmic lesson plan."

"What are you babbling about?" said Mary. Flo and I just want to make a lot of money by selling a lot of pretzels."

Flo chimed in, "Can you help us be more successful doctor?"

Off knew what the problem was that the girls had low self-esteem, due to guilt and shame tracing to childhood. Mary had concluded that money was hard to get and scarce. Flo had a lot of money once, but felt unworthy of it. They had to change their mind about themselves and the nature of the universe, especially vis-a-vis money. The question in his mind was how to present it in a way that would be palatable to the girls. A great psychiatrist named Dr. Milton Erickson had suggested that you must invent a new therapy for each patient. These girls didn't need Freudian or cognitive theories. They needed language that would make sense to them.

Despite their low self-esteem and negative beliefs about money, they knew that they were beautiful and that men drooled over them. So Hans started with that.

"So Flo, Mary, are you aware that men are attracted to you?"

"Yeah!," they replied in unison. "Men are constantly staring at us and undressing us with their eyes!"

"Well then, would you say that you are man magnets?"

"Abolutely," they replied.

"Well than all you have to do is become money magnets!"

"What do you mean doctor?"

"You see ladies, there is something called the "law of attraction." Just like men are attracted to pretty ladies like you, money is attracted to people who assume it is good, they deserve it, and are open to it. Just like a magnet attracts metal, money magnets attract money. Sometimes it just shows up…but usually you just have to work for it and it comes. Are you game?"

"Sure, what do we do to turn on the man-ey magnet?…I mean money magnet?"

"You are getting the idea. First imagine how men are attracted to you, then declare your worthiness to receive money, then just tap the top of your head and say…"*I am a money magnet!*" By now, the girls were laughing.

"You mean that's all we have to do?"

"No, you have to really believe that you are worthy of having a comfortable life, you have to be willing to share the money when you get it, you have to give to charity and homeless people for example. You have to start seeing the abundance in the world. You have to be willing to do your part in helping those who do not know about this yet to buy into it. This can even help those in poverty to gradually get out of it. You will be teaching others how to own their own power to help themselves. Once the money magnet helps you, it can gradually help millions all over the world."

The girls were stunned. But somehow they were able to accept Off's goofy statements. They began to furiously tap the top of their heads, affirming, "I am a money magnet." Off was beginning to see that he had to use New Age principles to help his patients, even if they were imaginary characters. He knew that the two girls would never be the same.

Off knew that the money magnet exercise would help the girls. But he also knew the danger of using spiritual principles like the "law of attraction" for strictly material gain. That is why he emphasized that some of the money must also be donated, given away to worthy causes. In the best case scenario, the girls would realize that all of material reality is part of God. That is why it is abundant. In order to tap into the abundance spiritual values would have to be embraced. Self-esteem would then be based upon the "real self, as" Dr. Karen Horney hypothesized.

A false sense of puffery gained by thinking the ego self can now make oodles of money is not the point. In fact, the misuse of the money magnet idea is a big obstacle to attaining the Great Cosmic Lesson Plan.

"People need to know that they are part of the oneness of the pure loving energy of spirit" thought Off. As usual, dealing with his patient's problems was helping him to articulate his own spiritual/psychological philosophy. As soon as Off was ready to understand life better, a new patient would arrive to help Hans further evolve his cognitive spiritual psychology. He knew that thoughts, powered by beliefs create "reality." Off was just waiting for the next patient. He was sure that he was very close to enlightenment. In fact, a new patient had just arrived. His name was Leo.

CHAPTER 18

The Big Bang Theory

Leo walked in with a grin on his face. He was a tall lanky man with dreadlocks. As usual, Off asked what his presenting problem was. Leo answered that he had an uncontrollable, irrational fear of cats. It seemed that his three roommates were trying to force him to accept an orphaned cat from one room-mate's deceased uncle Schrodinger. Schrodinger's cat was the great, great, great, grandson of the cat in the famous experiment of 1935. It seems that Uncle Schrodinger's father was a physicist. He devised an experiment that tested whether a cat, placed in a box was alive or dead. He might have died due to the deterioration of a random radioactive pellet.

It seems that all of Leo's roommates wanted to re-do the experiment. Leo did not give a crap about the experiment. He just wanted the cat out of the apartment. Off did not know much about quantum physics. All he knew was that if a phobic person is gradually exposed to the feared object, the fear tends to dissipate. Leo, on the other hand, did know about quantum physics. He explained that quantum physics sees a connection between energy and matter. Like Einstein, he saw an inter-play between the two. Einstein said that neither energy nor matter can be created or destroyed. Dr. Off immediately flashed on his own fear of death. If Einstein was right, all matter, including him would return to energy and back again. So there was nothing to be afraid about. Leo was irrationally afraid of cats, just as Off was irrationally afraid of death. If he could cure Leo, maybe he could find a cure for his own phobia!

Leo loved to pontificate and therapy was no exception. He thought he knew everything and was smarter than anyone else, especially his equally brilliant roommates. He was particularly humiliated that despite his knowledge of the new physics, Taoism, Hinduism and Zen Buddhism, he was still afraid of a cute, cuddly cat! He quoted the physicist David Bohm to Off. "The inseparable quantum interconnectedness of the whole universe is the fundamental reality and thus, relatively independently behaving parts are merely particular and contingent forms within the whole." Leo then screamed, "So if I am really one with the universe, why does that cat terrify me!"

Off pondered his response, he know that Leo's intellectual understanding of the universe was probably right, but Leo didn't get it in his heart. He told Leo that he was right but needed an experience of this interconnected Oneness between Leo and Schrodinger's cat! Dr. Off suggested that he and Leo meditate together. Leo was resistant to the idea. Yet, he was desperate to feel better. Off put on some soft, New Age music and instructed Leo to just follow his breath and observe his thoughts, no judgment. The music played, Leo drifted into a deep trancelike state. He felt a feeling of love, peace and oneness with every separate thing. Then he awakened and saw Off was doing a game show imitation. Off said, "The Final big payoff question is, What is the best way to overcome a cat phobia?" Leo stated, "the answer is to become one with the cat." "That is correct sir, replied Dr. Off pretending to be a talk show host."

Leo, you see, had had a vision during his meditation. He had walked into the apartment, imagined himself becoming one with the cat and felt a sense of peace. Yet, he also knew that he, Leo, was quite separate from the cat. He could now cope better with his cat phobia as well as the vicissitudes of life. He somehow knew now that all creation is really one, even though everyday experience tells us otherwise. The loving, peaceful Oneness-the source of all being, is our true nature. Fear comes up when we see a threat from the seeming "other." That was what war was all about. But when we experience the simultaneous oneness and separateness, fear is dissolved into peaceful and loving feelings. Leo awoke with absolutely no fear of cats.

Off was grinning from ear to ear. He had guided his patient into the oneness. The result was a complete cure. Not only was the cat-phobia cured but Leo seemed enlightened. Words can take you only so far in therapy and in life. The real healing comes to all of us as we allow the *experience* of the interplay of energy and matter. He knew that Leo would need more work on meditation, but he was on the right track. As the Dalai Lama once said, "Be the peace you want to see." On top of all that, Off got paid $200 for teaching Leo the truth! Leo gave Off a big hug and agreed to return the next week.

Off felt so peaceful, he knew he was on the right track of curing his own fear of death! Life was good, but he had to keep meditating to experience it. He and Leo were both on the road to enlightenment! Off knew now by experience that all humans are in the same boat. We are all deluded by the fear, anger and guilt of dealing with "others!" The apparent duality between self and others does make life seem scary. But the experience of oneness in meditation and eventually in all waking hours is the essence of the Great Cosmic Lesson Plan!

CHAPTER 19

Hans Off Accepts Life As It Is

Hans Off now knew he was not crazy. He was not schizophrenic. The voices he was hearing were some sort of spiritual guides. They were helping him to achieve inner peace. They were giving him an ineffable knowledge. All of his experiences were divinely inspired, designed to teach him his great cosmic lesson plan. It didn't matter that he seemed wacky to others. He began to see a new "transpersonal" psychologist, Dr. H. A. Shem. Dr. Shem took him to the same peaceful place he had taken Leo. Off learned that laughing, peace and love were good. He learned that he could still get angry at times-but he just had to let it go quickly. He had a tremendous positive transference to Dr. Shem. He wanted to be just like him, slow to anger and quick to forgive.

Dr. Off had attained a sense of peace that was hard to put into words. His life was good. All life is good. He learned something from all his patients. He learned from all the characters in his life. He learned to laugh without a laugh track. He learned not to take himself too seriously. He learned to tap into God's great abundance. He learned to share the abundance and how to tap into it with others. He learned to make good decisions, to control many aspects of his life. He learned that he was not in control of everything. He learned that it was a good thing he wasn't in control of everything. He learned to let go of anger, fear and guilt rather quickly. He learned never to harbor grudges. He was gradually even letting go of his grudge against Walter O'Malley, who moved his beloved

Brooklyn Dodgers to Los Angeles in 1958. He learned to let go of his fear of death. He learned to create as many win-win situations as he could. He was a happy man and all he wanted to do was share the happiness with others. As a certain pig used to say, "Th-th-th-that's all folks!"

AUTHOR BIO

Sam Menahem, Ph.D. is a spiritually oriented psychologist in Fort Lee N.J. He founded the Center for Psychotherapy and Spiritual Growth. He integrates humor and music into therapy, as well as prayer, meditation and hypnosis. He believes that we all have a spiritual core which is hidden by guilt, anger and fear. He helps people to let go of these core emotional blockages and the negative beliefs that go with them. He is the author of two previous books, *"When Therapy Isn't Enough: The Healing Power of Prayer and Psychotherapy"* and *"All Your Prayers Are Answered."* He is Adjunct Assistant Professor of Psychology at Columbia University and past president of the Association for Spirituality and Psychotherapy in New York City. He is a frequent lecturer and makes many radio and TV appearances. Web site, www.drmenahem.com, smenahem47@gmail.com,222 Bridge Plaza South #590, Fort Lee, N.J. 07024, (201) 944-1164.

ACKNOWLEDGEMENTS

There are so many people to thanks for the creation of this book. I have a wonderful wife, Susan, who helped me so much with the legal and practical issues of this book, Special thanks to my wonderful talented daughter who had the perspicacity to ask me, "What is life is for anyway?" at nine years of age! Thank you Lauren! And thank you for designing the beautiful cover of this book. Thank you to my brother Lewie and extended family for their support of this project. I thank my many loving, supportive friends, the people I have known since childhood, the gym guys, the poker guys (who have to listen to all of my jokes). I particularly thank my friend and colleague Michael Isaacs, who off handedly suggested I put together the many articles I wrote for the ASP (Association for Spirituality and Psychotherapy) Newsletter into a book. Special thanks to Bruce Kerievsky, my co-editor of the Newsletter for many of the suggested topics, which became chapters in this book. Also thanks to Diana Kerievsky, the Executive Director of ASP for many years. I thank my editor, Nora Isaacs for her editing, and fine tuning of the manuscript. Finally, I thank my father, Victor Menahem for giving me the "writing" gene. He was a fine writer himself and is quoted in the book.

REFERENCES

A Course in Miracles, Foundation for Inner peace, Tiburon California.1976.

Becker, Ernest, *The Denial of Death,* Free Press, 1988.

Benson, Herbert-*Timeless Healing: The Power and Biology of Belief,* Fireside Books, New York, 1996.

Bohm, David, Summary of his ideas-Wikkipedia-the Free Encyclopedia, 2014.p1.

Brenner, Charles, **An Outline of Psychoanalysis,** W.W. Norton, New York, 1989.

Byrne, Rhonda, *The Secret,* Atria Books, New York, 2006.

Carrington, Patricia, *Freedom in Meditation,* Doubleday, Anchor Press, N.Y.1977.

Collier, Robert, *The Secret of the Ages,* New York, 1926.

Crane, Larry, *The Sedona Method: The Release Technique,* Sedona Institute, Torrent Press, 1992.

Cranston, S. and Williams, R., *Reincarnation: A New Horizon in Science, Religion and Society*, Julian Press, New York, 1984.

de Laszlo, Violet S., **The Basic Writings of C,G. Jung**, Modern Library, New York, 1959.

Dwoskin, Hale, *The Sedona Method: The Key to Lasting Success, Peace and Emotional Well Being*, Sedona Press, Sedona Arizona, 1994.

Dyer, Wayne, *Real Magic*, Harper Collins, New York, 1992.

Erickson, Milton, *The Nature of Hypnosis and Suggestion*, Irvington Publishers, New York, 1980.

Frankl, Viktor, *Man's Search for Meaning*, Beacon Press, New York, 2006.

Hora, Thomas, *Healing through Spiritual Understanding*, pamphlet-PAGL.org.

Horney, Karen, *Neurosis and Human Growth*, W. W. Norton, New York,1951.

Huxley, Aldous, *The Perennial Philosophy*, Harper, Colophon Books, 1950.

Kushner, Harold, *When Bad Things Happen to Good People*, Random House, New York, 1981.

Maltz, Maxwell, *Psycho-cybernetics*, Psycho-cybernetics Foundation, New York, 1960.

Menahem, Sam, "*The Great Cosmic Lesson Plan*" *Pure Inspiration Magazine*, Fall 2008, pp93-96.

Reich Charles, *The Greening of America, Three Rivers Press, 1970*

Roberts, Jane *The Nature of Personal Reality*, Prentice Hall, Englewood Cliffs, N.J. 1976.

Rogers, Carl, *Client Centered Therapy*, Riverside Press, Cambridge Ma. 1951

Tillich, Paul, *The Courage To Be*, Yale University Press, New Haven CT. 1952.

Wapnick, Kenneth, *Fifty Miracle Principles*, Foundation for a Corse in Miracles, Riverside Ca. 1988.

Weiss, Brian, *Many Lives, Many Masters*, Hay House, Carlsbad Ca., 1988.

APPENDIX

Some techniques for self-healing

There are two ways of thinking-choose one
Read from top to bottom-pick one column to guide your life.
God, Source, Ground of being

Ego	Soul (higher self)
Selfish	Selfless
"I want what I want"	"I accept what I get"
"I want to be right."	"I want to be happy."
Anger, fear, guilt	Peace, love, joy
Omg	Om

Each time you are angry, fearful, guilty, or depressed, ask yourself which voice you are listening to? As soon as you realize you are listening to the ego, switch back to the soul, your real self! You will be surprised how quickly your bad mood lifts.

Here is another variation of the exercise above. Picture a little devil on your left shoulder-telling you what to do. Picture an angel on your right shoulder, also telling you what to do in whatever the situation is. The devil is the ego. Tell him to "shut the f--- up and turn to the right.

Do what the angel says. This technique is a variation of many 1950s cartoons I watched as a child.

Forgiving a parent

Picture your mother or father as a little kid. See one of your grandparents mistreating, abusing or ignoring the parent. Compassionately feel the pain of your parent. Realize that whatever they did to you was caused by their childhood wounds. Picture your parent and give them a big hug and say to yourself. "I forgive you." Breathe a deep sigh of relief.

Letting go of any resentment or fear or unworthiness

Open your hands as if throwing something away-say, "Let go." Then, turn your hands upward and say, "let go, let God." Then, raise your hands upward and say, "I accept healing."

Now do the same exercise, using acronyms, using the same motions. So you say, "lg, lglg, ah!!!" Now laugh at how funny it all seems and really let go of the problematic feeling or issue.